THE IRONIC LINK

THE IRONIC LINK

How Comedy Overcomes Depression

Felix Dey

NEW DEGREE PRESS
COPYRIGHT © 2021 FELIX DEY
All rights reserved.

THE IRONIC LINK
How Comedy Overcomes Depression

ISBN
978-1-63730-683-3   *Paperback*
978-1-63730-773-1   *Kindle Ebook*
979-8-88504-033-4   *Digital Ebook*

*To my mom Iris and stepdad Christian for
always letting me chase my dreams.*

To my future ex-wife—I've heard you're into writers.

CONTENTS

INTRODUCTION — 11

PART 1   **THE CASE FOR COMEDY** — 21
CHAPTER 1   THE SCIENCE OF DEPRESSION — 23
CHAPTER 2   UNMASKING YOUR TRUE SELF — 37
CHAPTER 3   DEPRESSION'S UGLY FACE — 51

PART 2   **THE WEIRDO IN THE ROOM** — 65
CHAPTER 4   THE HISTORY OF COMEDY — 67
CHAPTER 5   FEELING HOMESICK AT HOME — 79
CHAPTER 6   GO HEAL YOURSELF — 93

PART 3   **COMEDY IS FUNNY…AND SO MUCH MORE** — 107
CHAPTER 7   THE C IN COMEDY IS FOR CONNECTION — 109
CHAPTER 8   COMEDY IS FUNNY…AND SO MUCH MORE — 121
CHAPTER 9   HUMOR IS HOW WE ALL SURVIVE — 137

ACKNOWLEDGMENTS — 145
APPENDIX — 149

*You're only given a little spark of madness.
Don't ever lose that 'cause it keeps you alive.*

—ROBIN WILLIAMS

INTRODUCTION

> "Comedy has a way of normalizing just about any issue. When you can see tragedy through the lens of the ridiculous and the absurd, it doesn't define you anymore. When you make fun of your fears, it takes all the power out of it. Developing my sense of humor is one thing in my life that makes the most sense out of all of it. Because when you're in humor, you're present to the whole picture."
>
> —Adam Barnhardt

My first ever comedy teacher, Adam Barnhardt, used standup not only as a way to escape from, but also to cope with the hardships he has been through. It was humor, and more specifically, telling jokes that helped him through drug addiction, mental illness, dealing with his sexuality, and trying to fit into social norms. I interviewed Adam and many other comedians for my book to show how effective and *funny* it can be to take something serious and twist it ever so slightly to alleviate the pain and find an effective way to deal with it.

Starting out in comedy and taking my first standup class, my expectations were that I would see a bunch of funny people saying funny things and learning from their wittiness and humor. But I quickly realized not one person in this room didn't talk about their unique personal challenges, and to a certain extent, it was like "comedy therapy" because it helped me realize what mental health conditions were.

SMILE OF PAIN

There is one extraordinary group of people we can learn a lot from. It's a unique society processing its psychological issues out loud and who found a way to openly talk about it without being put into a box: standup comics. Of course, it is not scientifically proven that the extra-funny people in our society are more depressed than their average-funny counterparts. However, standup comics are just talking publicly about it to a bigger audience. If you want to understand someone going through depression but don't want to read through research papers or are too scared to talk to that person directly, look at how comedians handle it.

Imagine someone with a broken arm. Maybe you have had a sprained ankle or torn Achilles tendon yourself at one point. Maybe you're even reading this book with a fractured bone right now. Even though I never broke any part of my body (knock on wood), I could relate to someone who did, as I could see the plaster cast or crutches. I see the limitations and restrictions this person has due to that specific injury. However, why is it then that so many of us cannot or do not want to see and relate to a disease such as depression only because it's not physically noticeable?

And yes, some may say you can't see a disease like cancer either. But you certainly can see the physical effects cancer has on someone's body. It is as insidious as depression or any other mental health condition. In a way, depression is mental cancer. Curable when detected early enough, but the risk it might come back is always present.

COMEDIANS CAN'T REALLY BE SUFFERING, RIGHT?

Let me clarify at this point of the book what the difference is between a comic and a comedian, as the terms are often used interchangeably and usually defined in terms of each other.

While there are many differing opinions about what the exact difference between a comic and comedian is, I found it to be true that being a comic refers to someone who does live, solo standup comedy routines. On the other hand, being a comedian can refer to someone who might do standup but might also do improv or sketch comedy. The implied difference is that comics only perform in the one venue of standup. A comedian is a much broader term that refers to someone who performs comedic material to elicit laughs. For example, this can be accomplished by acting in movies. To put it short: A comic is a comedian; a comedian isn't necessarily a comic.

Standup comedians are hilarious (most of them, at least). Their whole purpose is to think and write about something funny, make others laugh, and help their audience escape from their daily struggles for five, ten, or sixty-plus minutes. So, they can't really be the ones suffering, right? Yet if the clown makes everyone laugh, who will make the clown laugh?

> "One of the things that I realized in the course of doing it [standup comedy] is how much my coming to grips with stuff was realizing that I'm not gonna beat this [depression]. I'm not gonna win. I don't get to erase this part of my brain. It's there, so I just have to learn to live with it, face it down, and navigate my life with it."
>
> —Chris Gethard

Chris Gethard, known for his HBO comedy special "Career Suicide" is a person who has been living on the fine ledge between tragedy and comedy all his life. He is a comedian, and he is living with this inner demon called depression. I use the term demon because depression is something that cannot be physically described. It is something so subtle and elusive yet destructive and, in some cases, fatal. Being in his forties now, Chris accepted this inner demon will always be a part of him. He doesn't suffer from depression anymore—nor is it something he is cured of. Instead, it is just a "thing" he has to manage.

As Chris came to terms with his own illness, he began to see similar patterns of behavior and coping mechanisms surfacing in conversations with other comedians who struggled with the disease. Chris saw tremendous comfort and community could be found in open dialogue about these shared experiences and that humor had a unique power.

THE UMBRELLA OF MENTAL HEALTH

There is nothing funny about depression. It is a debilitating illness that, at its worst, robs its victims of peace of mind, self-esteem, and in extreme cases, their lives. Still, so many of us struggle to understand mental disorders in others. I had a hard time myself grasping it in the past. I've always heard people talking about mental health issues. I saw it on the news when yet another celebrity opened up about his or her mental well-being, or rather, ill-being.

I hear family members or friends using words like "depression" and "anxiety" in their daily vocabulary. In a sense, these two specific terms that revolve around mental health issues, the two "common colds" of personal disorder, are being used very lavishly in today's society to express a general feeling of sadness. Looking back, I catch myself using these terms interchangeably and very loosely as well.

It wasn't until I started performing standup comedy with people talking about their own mental agonies, that I finally made sense of it. I realized we can understand depression in others and ourselves by following the psyche of the comic. These people live on the ultimate line between comedy and tragedy, which is where mental health issues linger. What I have found through my research and interviews with comedians, psychiatrists, and therapists offered me a unique insight into living with our inner demons.

Everybody experiences feelings of sadness or anxiety throughout life. Without sadness and sorrow, we would have a hard time defining happiness. It grounds us, and, to some extent, is even healthy for our bodies and minds. Sadness is a vital emotional response to pain that alerts us to how we need to treat ourselves and how we want to be treated by others.

Depression, on the other hand, is a chronic mood disorder. The umbrella of depression encompasses a major depressive disorder and its related psychological distress including bipolar disorder, postpartum depression, post-traumatic stress syndrome, anxiety disorder, and suicide. Or to put it in the most straightforward terms: Depression is an illness that requires treatment.

WHAT WE CAN LEARN FROM DEPRESSION'S STIGMA

As I'm writing this book right now, a pandemic runs across our planet. Of the coronavirus' many side effects, perhaps the least appreciated are psychological. The World Health Organization (WHO) stated that in the Americas (North and South America), this psycho-social crisis has become its own epidemic. According to the Centers for Disease Control and Prevention, depression is the leading cause of disability in the United States for individuals ages fifteen to forty-four. In 2020, the *Washington Post* reported that in the US, the national rate of anxiety tripled in the second quarter of 2020 compared to the same period in 2019 (from 8.1 percent to 25.5 percent). Depression almost quadrupled (from 6.5 percent in 2019 to 24.3 percent in 2020).

According to the WHO, globally, more than 264 million people of all ages suffer from depression. This means over 3 percent of the entire world population is suffering (and partly dying) from a disease that is still so hard to understand and grasp for those not directly affected by it.

However, the ones going through and battling this disease remain among the most stigmatized groups. The tragic results from these biases can range from reluctance to seek help, lack of understanding by family, friends, and others, to health systems that don't adequately cover mental illness treatments. Certain beliefs also accompany these prejudices such as feeling you will never succeed at certain challenges or neither you nor anybody else can improve your situation.

Precisely because of these reasons, the majority experiencing a mental disorder shy away from openly talking about it or at least sharing it with a loved one. This behavior led to what some people refer to as "smiling depression." While smiling depression is not a technical term psychologists use, it is certainly possible to be depressed and manage to successfully mask the symptoms.

"All it takes is a beautiful fake smile to hide an injured soul and they will never notice how broken you really are."

—ROBIN WILLIAMS

COMICS ARE THE ULTIMATE TIGHTROPE WALKERS

Understanding how to live, laugh, and love others with mental health conditions is not left only for therapists, psychologists, or people directly affected by it. The main purpose of this book is to make a compelling argument for comics as the ultimate tightrope walkers and how you or someone you know can apply comedy to cope with psychological struggles.

Comics flourish on the fine line between humor and depression, comedy and tragedy, sanity and insanity. Through the lens of the comedian, we can empathize, understand, and even relate to others struggling with their inner demons.

This book will work as a steppingstone along the path to establishing compassion, insights, and an exciting understanding of mental health. Maybe not overnight, but over time. If you or someone close to you is battling this vicious condition, the people and suggested tools in this book can help you filter pain through humor so it will hurt increasingly less day after day.

The Ironic Link will bring you closer to understanding mental disorders such as depression in others and yourself and help you be more empathetic and sympathetic. It is time to finally talk about a devastating condition that is too often swept under the rug and help the ones in need.

PART 1

THE CASE FOR COMEDY

CHAPTER 1

THE SCIENCE OF DEPRESSION

―

Depression. The silent pandemic.

As a comedian, a compelling voice urges you not to ruin the image people have of you by openly revealing how sad you are. Yet a standup routine can be a unique vehicle to make the world around the suffering less painful. Going on stage is the one salvation as you can use your inner pain as the fuel to channel a joke and make yourself feel better. We comedians balance this narrow ridge between having our audience laugh with or at us when amusingly exposing our sorrow. In an episode of Marc Maron's podcast show "WTF" in 2010, he speaks with Robin Williams about how hard it can be for a comic to decide how far to go with an audience—how personal, and sometimes dark, you can allow yourself to be.

"You have to be funny about it to get out of this," Williams says, "and I'm going to find *it*, and you [the audience] are going to help me find it to break through and release me from my misery." However, if Robin Williams, one of the most admired comedians of our time, ends his own life, it's a painful reminder of how powerful mental agonies can be. It's a reminder that profound emotional anguish can occur in the talented, the successful, the funniest.

Everyone knows it exists, but only a few really understand where depression and other psychological diseases are coming from. It is as much a social disease as it is biological. Mental health experts around the world agree that the problem is neither purely of genetic nature nor sociological. Yet, the common belief that major depression and anxiety disorder are caused by a chemical imbalance in our brains outweighs the impression that it is as much a social and psychological imbalance.

You won't find a scientist saying depression is purely a biological phenomenon, says Johann Hari, Swiss-Scottish journalist and author featured during Joe Rogan's "The Joe Rogan Experience" podcast. Just as depression has social causes, it requires social as well as individual solutions.

According to a 2018 study from Purdue University, the ideal income point in the US for emotional well-being is between $60,000 and $75,000. Interestingly enough, when people earned more than $105,000, their happiness levels decreased. As this study shows that more money doesn't make us happier, it also won't prevent us from feeling depressed, respectively.

Yet, our society considers materialistic and monetary values as the main drivers for our overall contentment. We tend to compare ourselves with false expectations and spend most of our lives talking about statuses. Right after we were born, we signed a social contract before even knowing how to read and write. An agreement that determines what makes us happy and where to find contentment based on the cultural standards we are born in. We feed off a kind of junk food for both mind and soul. We get conditioned where to find bliss and what it looks like. You or I can have everything we could want by our society's norms. Still, most people's standards (particularly in Western cultures) need to be overhauled.

For countless individuals, it is more important where they are standing socially than improving their own trajectory. As human beings, we need more than comparing numbers on our bank accounts and showing off with job titles.

JUNK VALUES
Just like junk food doesn't meet our nutritional needs (it may be temporarily satisfying but quickly fades away and makes us feel sick), junk values don't meet our psychological needs, and they take us away from a good life, says Johann Hari who published the book *This Could Be Why You're Depressed or Anxious* in 2019. What we need is a fulfilling life, a life of meaning and purpose.

Dr. Michael Mah, psychiatrist at the UCLA Department of Psychiatry, confirms this belief. In a personal interview, he explained to me every human being requires four psychological needs to feel well.

- A meaningful connection to other people
- A sense of purpose
- A sense of community
- Meaningful work

Today's society is becoming increasingly worse in meeting these basic needs. It is no surprise then that diagnoses of major depression in the US have risen dramatically by 33 percent since 2013, a report done by Blue Cross Blue Shield reveals. Consequently, as the problem goes deeper than just a lack in chemicals and hormones, the solutions need to become much broader, too.

TRIBAL LIVING: HOW COMMUNITY RELIEVES DEPRESSION

But maybe we don't have to look ahead and be compulsively innovative to find a solution. Maybe we need to look back thousands of years ago and understand how our ancestors used to live. Dr. Mah subscribes to the idea that we are still human beings just like 10,000 years ago when we lived in tribes. This herd mentality is still deep-seated in our ancient brains. However, our DNA hasn't caught up to the socialization, or rather de-socialization and society we're living in now.

If we look at demographics of people who have a strong sense of community such as Mormon or Jewish people, the incidence and prevalence of depression is strikingly much lower than in other communities. A higher sense of belonging is consequently directly related to less depressive episodes and fewer suicidal thoughts (Fisher et al., 2015).

Loneliness is a killer.

Living in tribes thousands of years ago, if a human got separated, the possibility of survival ran automatically toward zero. Being alone, this individual might either be attacked and eaten by a wild animal, freeze, or starve to death. Hence, the reason someone feels hyper-anxious or depressed when separated from the tribe is that they will die unless they are reconnected. Those mechanisms are still very much alive in us today. Our bodies may have caught up over time, it takes a while, though, for our DNA to advance accordingly.

The way we live can be transcribed in the genes of our offspring. The interesting part is these gene expressions can be turned on and off, depending on the environment around us. Suppose someone has a disposition toward a mood disorder because someone in that person's family was diagnosed with depression. Under the right circumstances, that person will experience the same conditions. This is something that, in some ways, is written in the code of our genes. At the same time, it also means then that the right context can suppress the expression of these particular genes and prevent mental illnesses from developing in the first place.

ARE ANTI-DEPRESSANTS THE BE ALL END ALL?
To this day, mental health experts still argue about the best approaches to treat depression and anxiety. It has not been proven yet, and may never be, that a deficiency of serotonin is the single cause of mental distress. Serotonin is a chemical that nerve cells produce that regulates our mood, emotions, attention, and is responsible for our overall well-being.

Getting to the bottom of someone's psychological agony has to be evaluated case by case, as every single one is unique. Yet, making sense of the different causes will help find better treatments and slowly remove the stigma that mental health illnesses have long carried. Today's Western psychiatrists are quick to subscribe antidepressants. It is not entirely their fault, though, and for many people, it does indeed represent the best treatment.

> *"Taking antidepressants to cope with depression is like having floaties on in a pool. It's going to prevent you from sinking, but it won't swim to the other end of the pool for you."*
>
> —MICHAEL MAH, PHD

Medication for depression is not going to make the lasting, meaningful changes in one's life that will lead to a long-term improvement in mood, let alone happiness. It is rather a Band-Aid approach than a permanent solution. It does prevent those affected from falling into the depths of despair temporarily. It can certainly lighten the load on that person and make him or her a little bit more motivated to get up and go, but that same person still has to swim to the end of the pool.

On the one hand, antidepressants are proven to work and very popular. They will make the patient feel better. Chemically, they will help that person ruminate less before going to bed so he or she can get a better night's sleep. On the other hand, there is also a significant placebo effect, which is crucial to improving overall emotional health. It is a person's expectation that a specific treatment can work even though it might not have demonstrable effects. Our bodies' own chemistry can then cause those effects we have expected in the first place. Placebo is basically the body's ability to heal itself.

Really getting to the bottom of what's making somebody sad and anxious requires a two-hour evaluation at minimum, says Dr. Mah. Humans are complex beings, and understanding what makes a person feel a certain way is complicated and involves a process. However, in order to treat most people efficiently, prescribing antidepressants will stop the disease temporarily from doing greater harm. Still, dressing a deep flesh wound will only alleviate the pain on the surface, if at all.

There is no doubt the best approach is a combination of medication and talk-therapy. Medication will have a more or less immediate effect on a patient's mood. At the same time, talk-therapy will help them see the light at the end of the tunnel in the long run. It will help a patient pull herself out of that hole of despair and hopelessness. Yet, 56.4 percent of American adults with a mental illness received no treatment, according to a report from Mental Health America. This means that in 2019, over twenty-four million individuals who have suffered through a mental health illness didn't undergo any therapy, let alone healing.

This is undoubtedly a system issue. Psychiatrists these days face a great challenge: Getting to the core of somebody when all they have are thirty-minute medication tracks or forty-five-minute intakes can only help so much. A psychiatric intake process is a form of negotiated interaction, where patient presentations are affected by a referral source, the illness itself, and its behavior. Hence, getting to the bottom of somebody's mental condition(s) is left to the therapist unless the person has a psychiatrist who practices holistically, which is even harder to find.

Our health system is not built for psychiatrists to have enough time to effectively get into the patient's mind and history like a therapist would do. That is why therapy has to some extent been shifted over to the therapist alone. In contrast, medication management has been left to the psychiatrist.

The system's problem is that by 2025, the US will have a shortage of psychiatrists, mental health counselors, psychologists, and school counselors, The Substance Abuse and Mental Health Services Administration estimates.

Recently, attempts to de-stigmatize mental health has resulted in many new patients who are brave enough to seek help. The COVID-19 pandemic has produced a tremendous number of patients as well. People who were once healthy face great struggles due to circumstances forced on them during the pandemic. Therefore, it is also a supply and demand issue. The gap between the number of providers and people who need help becomes progressively wider.

Eventually, professional therapy in the US will become successively harder to find. Wait times can be anywhere between three weeks and a year—valuable time that can mean, in the most severe cases, the difference between life and death. For that reason, people are trying to find other ways to cope with their psychological distress.

COMEDY: DEFENSIVE POSTURE, CREATIVE ENDEAVOR, OR BOTH?

"Comedy can often be a defensive posture against depression."

—DR. DEBORAH SERANI

Dr. Serani is a clinical psychologist I spoke to who treats entertainers with depression in New York City. It comes to no surprise then that many people in the arts, like comedians, found their creative outlet to be a coping mechanism for their struggle with depression and anxiety. Anyone who uses humor through personal struggles and tragedies already has a higher developed sense of managing their mental health.

Back when I was starting standup comedy, I quickly understood the importance of reaching people and telling a relatable story. I realized how standup could become a great form of therapy. However, the sad clown is a dangerous stereotype, Dr. Serani emphasized. Although it is a common belief that all comedians struggle to some extent with mental health, it is definitely not always the case.

Maybe percentagewise, comedians aren't more depressed than the rest of society. Maybe the rest of society just isn't talking about it professionally, says Chris Gethard, American comedian, actor, and writer (Comedians Tackling Depression, 2019).

Yes, many people in the expressive arts do struggle with depression. Dr. Kay Redfield Jamison, clinical psychologist, and bestselling author even proves the relationship between art and madness in her book *Touched with Fire*. Yet, many of these people who happen to be comedians find humor to be a healthy defense.

Crafting amusing and entertaining material requires a lot of deep thinking to eventually find "the funny" in it. This doesn't mean comedians are necessarily depressed, but they're just engrossed in their thoughts and want to work it through, whatever it takes. Whether it is their experiences, awareness, or personal struggles, the laughter is hidden in every aspect of our lives.

> "One of the things I've learned in working with very creative people is you cannot categorize anybody as being all the same, because they are extremely unique."
>
> —Dr. Deborah Serani

Using humor as a defense mechanism against depression and anxiety can become challenging and requires a lot of creative imagination as pain and sorrow is the source of your creativity. In general, people use two kinds of defenses:

1. Primitive defense mechanisms: In psychoanalytic theory, a primitive defense mechanism is a mechanism that protects against anxiety associated with the death instinct. It is the first to occur developmentally and tends to keep us very stuck, unhappy, and troubled in our life.

2. More highly adapted defense mechanisms: Highly adaptive defense mechanisms, such as humor, prove to help people better and sustainably cope through life. They allow us to function normally and act rationally.

COMEDIC MASTERY

What makes someone good at their craft? Zig Ziglar, a famous American author and motivational speaker, said in 1993:

> *"Repetition is the mother of learning, the father of action, which makes it the architect of accomplishment."*

Many comedians use this kind of repetition for their writing and performances. What started out as a mediocre joke can potentially evolve into a comedian's best piece. Very frequently, I catch myself saying, "Let me just rewrite it a little differently." Even if I'm not writing it, I am then performing it over and over again, whether it's on a bigger stage at a local comedy club, at an open-mic, or in front of family and friends. In the field of psychology, this is called *mastery*.

Mastery means someone can gradually improve, making that person feel good. Another way to say this would be a *therapeutic accomplishment*. That repetitive piece for comedians is considered a very healing event. In standup comedy, this repeated process comes along with an extreme work ethic. There is an intense, or even obsessive urge to find the funny. And it is through that pursuit that something curative must be happening. Most people don't have this pursuit and drive on a daily basis because it can also bring them to the point of despair.

PAIN AS A MOTIVATOR FOR CREATIVITY

> *"Pain often becomes a big motivator for creativity. I think that often people utilize the pain in a way that helps them create stories."*
>
> —DR. BENJAMIN HOULTBERG

Dr. Benjamin Houltberg is not only my former professor at USC business school but also a licensed therapist and the director of research at the USC Performance Science Institute. He points out that emotional pain can be both a great motivator and source for creativity, but it is not sustainable for two reasons.

1. First, pain is a motivator for people to change or think differently because adrenaline as well as cortisol, the stress hormone, is released in moments of tension or fear. In fact, many people never change until they feel a little pain. However, too much cortisol over a prolonged period can lead to mood swings, which show as anxiety, depression, or irritability, and physical conditions like rapid weight gain or high blood pressure, among others. Pain can ignite a mighty fire, but that fire is burning almost too much. It could consume them, and they can't hold that fire when it's emerged out of pain.

2. Second, there is a thin line in using pain as a motivator. It becomes challenging if people start healing from their pain. Once pain is healed, comedians in

particular will have a tough time figuring out where to get their drive and creativity from. This leaves many of them in a dilemma. They either force themselves back to these emotionally painful places, where they might fall on their faces again, or they end up in a healed state in which they start to question their purpose. They initially capitalized on their discomfort, transforming it into something funny and bearable. Without that as a source, they have no outlet for creating new material.

Only when the purpose can get integrated into the art can the comedian see an increase in performance again. If they find it, that spark then comes from a different place than before. It is fueled in a cleaner way. It is created from a more sustainable place instead from a source that causes damage along the way, both to the comedian and to the people around him or her.

Many comedians become what they are not because they've always been the class clown. In fact, if you think back to your school days, being the funny one in your class meant being popular and was also associated with having more friends. As I will show you in these next chapters, today's most famous comedians were outsiders and misfits. They became comedians precisely because they were unpopular and disliked. The high art of performing comedy can bring control, approval from friends and family, and prove to the outside world you are worthy of being listened to, understood, and liked. Pain and feelings of anger and anxiety are channeled into a comedic artistic expression that continues to bring joy and happiness to millions of people in our world.

CORE LESSONS

- Depression has social causes; it requires social solutions as well as individual solutions.

- Just like junk food doesn't meet our nutritional needs, junk values don't meet your psychological needs, and they take us away from a good life. What we need is a fulfilling life, a life of meaning and purpose.

- Placebo is the body's ability to heal itself.

- The reason someone feels hyper anxious or depressed when separated from the tribe is that they will die unless they are reconnected. Those mechanisms are still very much alive in us today.

- Medication for depression is not going to make the lasting, meaningful changes in one's life that will lead to a long-term improvement in mood.

- The best treatment is medication with talk-therapy combined.

- Anyone who uses humor through personal struggles and tragedies already has a greater developed sense of coping.

- *Therapeutic accomplishment.* That repetitive piece for comedians is considered a very healing event for them.

- Pain is a powerful motivator, but it's a destructive one in the long run and not sustainable for the human mind and body.

CHAPTER 2

UNMASKING YOUR TRUE SELF

"In my opinion, being able to both deliver and understand humor is an essential life skill."

—FELIX DEY

If you had asked me back then when I was still living in Germany whether I would ever end up performing standup or even writing a book about it, I would have laughed and called you crazy. I was the kind of guy who majored in economics at a renowned university, living in an environment where most of my friends wanted to get into private banking or consulting. Doing something creative was considered the hard outlier and viewed with a lot of skepticism. Artistic hobbies, let alone professions, were only left for natural talents. People were able to put them into this "artistic" box, whereas folks like me were always dancing around in a more conservative and ordinary one.

I came to Los Angeles to pursue my master's degree in Entrepreneurship & Innovation at the University of Southern California (USC). Even after moving there, I didn't mean to unleash my artful beast. Business and comedy? You can connect the dots already? Right, me neither. But it was my professor in my Design Thinking class who gave us an assignment that would change my life's trajectory entirely. He asked us to do something out of our comfort zone, something we had never done before. The only requirement, though, was that whatever we decided to do, it had to be somewhat tied to entrepreneurship.

After doing some research, I almost enrolled in a public speaking class to improve giving presentations and pitching business ideas. Luckily, I also came across an in-person standup comedy workshop in downtown LA. Of course, that public speaking class would equip me with the tools necessary to enhance my abilities to represent myself more effectively and professionally.

Yet, the idea to connect with an audience through humor and being able to entertain them ignited a spark in me that eventually turned into a bursting flame. I followed my gut feeling and enrolled, as it felt like the right thing to do, even though my parents and friends wouldn't take me seriously after I told them about it.

In fact, standup comedians and entrepreneurs have a lot in common. Similar to comedians, founders draw inspiration and new ideas from the most unexpected areas of life. And as the best business idea will never be successful if executed without great thought and consideration, the funniest joke will never make an audience laugh if delivered poorly. It was exciting to see how much constructing new comedic material resembles finding novel business concepts: If you force it, it won't happen. Or when it does, it'll most likely fail miserably.

The most important thing for an any entrepreneur is that her product or service is a must-have for her customers. Not a nice-to-have, because no one ever made money with something that is just nice to have. On the other hand, the joke needs to be funny to a comedian's audience. One could argue a great delivery could make up for a bad joke. But I can assure you out of personal experience, that is not the case, unless your name is Eddie Murphy or Tina Fey. Entrepreneurs are always looking for anomalies and opportunities in the world to come up with new ideas. Comedians always look for inspiration when observing themselves and others to incorporate them into material. Both comedians and entrepreneurs are explorers first, entertainers and businesspeople respectively second.

To the same extent, they look around and ask themselves: What seems odd? What requires attention that doesn't get enough? What is everyone annoyed by that people still do out of habit? For Travis Kalanick and Garrett Camp, founders of the technology platform and ride-sharing market leader Uber, it was the struggle to find a taxi in Paris on a snowy December night in 2008. They asked themselves: "Why can't you just request a ride simply by tapping your phone?" The next year, Uber officially launched and has been growing ever since.

Sebastian Maniscalco, one of the top five highest-earning standup comedians of 2019, observed and questioned Uber.

In 2016, he even opened his Netflix comedy special "Why Would You Do That?" with an entire skit about Uber:

> *"Uber is expanding into a lot of different areas. You don't have this yet here in New York City, but in Los Angeles, they have a thing called Uber Kitten, where they'll bring a cat to your house for one hour. Why would you do that? I've never been sitting around my home and asked my wife, "Babe, call Uber. Let's get a cat over here for one hour. I need to pet something."*

In my opinion, being able to both deliver and understand humor is an essential life skill. Whether it is for personal relationships, your mental health, setting the tone for a business meeting, or improving leadership skills, humor touches upon almost every facet of our lives.

THE POWER OF UNMASKING YOUR AUTHENTIC SELF

Authenticity is one of the most critical characteristics any comedian or entrepreneur requires to succeed. Both are storytellers. To have a story delivered effectively, whether it is to investors or a comedy club audience, we need to behave in a way consistent with our true underlying identity and values.

Our unique identity, though, is sometimes difficult to express and very fragile. For some people, it can be easily harmed by others and even themselves. Mental awareness plays a crucial role in determining who we are and what we stand for. It defines how we see the world and how the world sees us. Precisely because it is such a fragile thing, it can be easily broken and needs to be well-protected and constantly maintained.

However, without even realizing it, our psychological agility, or in a broader sense, mental health, is sometimes under attack. Whether the origins of our struggles are of chemical or sociological nature, this identity, or in technical jargon "comedic persona," is what makes each standup comedian differentiable and special. It is a distinctively incomparable voice.

Batman: *"If you're working alone, wear a mask."*

Robin: *"I'm not afraid to be seen standing up to these guys."*

Batman: *"The mask is not for you. It's to protect the people you care about."* (The Dark Knight Rises, 2012)

While Batman is wearing a mask to protect the ones he loves and cares about, a comedian's shield comes from the unmasking of oneself: being unafraid of judgment and fully vulnerable. This is how a persona is born and a voice is heard. A comedian's persona is derived from the core of his or her personality. It is about liberating one's individuality and being wholly oneself.

Yet, being yourself is easier said than done. Who really knows what their "selves" are? It requires a lot of internal work, but it is one of the greatest assets we have when framed correctly. Whether you are a comedian or not, ask yourself the following questions:

- What is important to me?

- What values do I live by?

- How do I express my beliefs through my thoughts and actions toward others?

Comedians pay attention to what is naturally making them and others laugh in life. Sometimes we crack up so hard about something in a particular situation, but it is almost impossible to replicate this moment and tell it to someone later. These bits are one source of your unique sense of humor.

Nevertheless, there is a difference between saying funny things and saying things in a way they are received as actually funny by others. The latter is a talent and aligns with a comedian's persona. It has an unparalleled style and point of view that will stick with an audience much longer. At the core, it is about thinking and delivering something ordinary and putting it into a completely different scenario or context to generate laughs. Through this approach, a comedian makes his or her audience look at a familiar topic from an entirely different angle, which is also called *observational comedy*.

As it all comes down to developing a robust comedic persona, half of all my standup comedy class exercises consisted of precisely doing that. In my very first session, we were asked to step on stage alone. My teacher would ask me a set of questions, which I then answered with a mic in my hand in front of my classmates. A few of these prompts were as follows:

- What does death mean to you?

- Where are you most vulnerable?

- Tell me about ten things you overcame in your life.

With his decade-long experience in teaching standup comedy and a highly developed sense of emotional intelligence (EQ), he could decipher my answers to get a feeling of where my sense of humor was coming from. At the same time, it was also an exercise and my first experience in opening up to strangers and showing my most vulnerable side. Watching my classmates doing it showed me how talking freely about mental health or just about any topic without judgment was a relief. Even though we had just met each other, you could already feel the robustness of the circle of trust we created in that first class.

INSANELY FUNNY

> *"Nobody can save you but yourself, and you're worth saving. It's a war not easily won, but if anything is worth winning then this is it."*
>
> —CHARLES BUKOWSKI

Living and working in the realms of standup comedy in a city like LA, I quickly saw how comedians are continuously fighting the war Bukowski is referring to. Bukowski himself, known for numerous poems and novels about life's struggles and staying true to your identity, spent a lifetime coping with manic depressions.

His mental health condition fundamentally influenced his writing. In *Screams from the Balcony*, a collection of letters illustrating Bukowski's life, he eloquently writes about his experience with the disease. Although his work was most popular from the early 1940s until he died in 1994, Bukowski's words still resonate with people today. And while it is still regarded as controversial by many, some argue that those affected by psychotic diseases like Bukowski undergo heightened creative powers that can mold into unparalleled art pieces.

For many of my comedy classmates, standup is therapy. Every class started with something called the *Clearing* process. During this activity, every student had to go on stage and talk about anything relevant to them. From how the week went to any concerns or worries we dealt with. For many of us, it was a comedic remedy after all.

For the first time in my life, I was a total newbie and felt like an outsider. It came with no surprise then that I wasn't jumping off my seat and volunteering to be the first for *Clearing*; it was my classmate Lauren who started us off. Lauren is a Jewish American girl born and raised in LA, living alone in her mid-thirties, who does some joke writing when she's not at work and spends parts of her free time on dating apps. But what she would share with us during our first class opened the door for me to a whole new world I never really paid attention to before. Lauren has bipolar disorder (or formerly known as manic-depressive illness or manic depression).

It blew my mind how, without batting an eye, Lauren opened up to a group of complete strangers and shared how she was being stalked by her mental illness almost her entire life. At the time, I had problems even sharing to new people what I had for dinner the night before, and here was Lauren taking the stage and explaining how at one point, she thought she was Jesus. That thought was terrifying for her, though, because she felt she had all this power being Jesus, but no one in this world should feel this mighty.

This was just one example of a typical psychosis episode she went through. Each mental health condition is unique. However, Lauren explained to me in a very easy-to-understand way what the illness does to her:

"It [psychosis] feels like you're dreaming out loud. You're saying things from your subconscious mind or a random place. Another way to describe it is that you feel like you're connecting the dots to random things in your life that don't make sense."

Lauren said the worst thing about her bipolar psychosis, despite acting strange and having severe mood disorders, was being taken to the hospital. Whereas going through depression doesn't require the patient to be hospitalized necessarily, experiencing severe mania episodes needs immediate professional help and medication. Every time she was admitted and felt isolated, she promised herself to do standup comedy once she got released.

"I just did it for fun to push myself and challenge myself. I never really thought I'd become a real standup comedian. It was just a way to break free from my life at the time, which was dictated by psychosis and depressive episodes," she adds.

Looking back at her manic disorder, Lauren can laugh it off. Although she is still depressed and experiences her highs and lows, she now thinks her stories of the mania taking over are hilarious. For example, she would get naked and randomly walk through the hospital halls because she felt she needed to rebirth herself. She is able to deliver stories like this in a very light-hearted and entertaining manner that neither herself nor the person listening feels uncomfortable. Performing comedy becomes very therapeutic for her. It is eye-opening and provides a lot of healing. She knew once she shared it with the world and made fun of it, nobody could use it against her.

Comedy brings light to situations like dating and being single that some people would typically become depressed about. Yet, the flip side of it is that Lauren is also crying about it when she is in therapy. But it is this vulnerability and authenticity that makes her a good standup comedian. In a way, she is a therapist for others. The student became the master. She wants others struggling with bipolar disorder to make light of their situation when watching her perform and tell her story.

I want to leave you with one last exercise we did as I believe it is something valuable for not only comedians but also for every human being. We called it the *mirror exercise*. Each of us had to step in front of a full-length mirror, look into our image, and pretend as if we were talking to another person. With confidence in your voice, the task was then to tell yourself, "*I forgive you for...*" ten times in a row for ten different reasons. I started by telling myself, "*I forgive you for not calling your grandparents as much as you should since you left Germany.*" Others stood up and said, "*I forgive you for dropping out of college,*" or "*I forgive you for trying to commit suicide as a teenager.*" I had only known these people for a little bit over an hour by then, but I already felt a bizarre yet powerful unity among us. It's precisely this unity with an audience that the best standup comedians in the world can achieve when performing on stage. It is authentic, honest, raw, and, most importantly, relatable.

Whether you feel well right now or find yourself in a dark place, I encourage you to give this exercise a try. All it requires is yourself, your thoughts, and a mirror. Everybody has one somewhere in their house or apartment. I don't want you to force yourself to think of exactly ten things you forgive yourself for, but we all have some demons, big or small, lingering in the back of our heads.

Saying those things out loud won't change the past, but it creates a place to confess your struggles and fears without judgment or punishment. Your past, present, and future will become more apparent as this exercise helps you gain control of your emotions and improves your overall mood. I often refer to it as advanced journaling. Writing down your thoughts is great, yet, saying them out loud toward your mirror image is the ultimate confrontation with what haunts you at night.

Why should you forgive yourself for something that's in the past anyway you're asking? Because if you can't even forgive yourself for your actions, how will you ever be able to forgive others? It is a practice that brings you closer to your negative thoughts, identifies your stressors, and helps you release that mental grip.

This exercise is so powerful and influential because people tend to be too hard on themselves. We sometimes talk to ourselves in a way we wouldn't speak to our worst enemy. Allowing us to recognize our mistakes and practice forgiveness can improve self-esteem, confidence, and overall mental health.

Standup is a way of seeing yourself from all perspectives. The irony behind it is you're an extrovert while becoming highly introspective. Comedy is helping me analyze where my issues are, where they're coming from, and what is happening around me, and I hope it will do the same for you.

CORE LESSONS
- Delivering and understanding humor is an essential life skill.

- Humor touches upon almost every facet of our lives: personal relationships, mental health, setting the tone for a business meeting, or improving leadership skills.

- To have a story delivered effectively, we need to behave in a way consistent with our true underlying identity and values.

- Our identity and values define how we see the world and how the world sees us.

- A comedian's shield comes from the unmasking of oneself: being unafraid of judgment and fully vulnerable.

- We sometimes talk to ourselves in a way we wouldn't speak to our worst enemy. By allowing us to recognize our mistakes and practice forgiveness, we can improve self-esteem, confidence, and overall mental health.

- Vulnerability and authenticity makes a good standup comedian.

- Comedy is a way of seeing yourself in all perspectives.

- Comedy is about facing the fear and anxiety of the unknown.

CHAPTER 3

DEPRESSION'S UGLY FACE

I lost my father when I was sixteen. Don't get me wrong, though; he's still alive and well (as far as I know) but dead to me since. In fact, the decision I made to cut him out of my life, more than a decade ago, laid the foundation for who I am today. To some extent, I even have to thank him for the ways he treated me when I was younger. It has taught me a great deal about resilience and mental toughness early on.

I am mentioning mental toughness here because it was during that time when I first had to be psychologically strong to escape an emotionally abusive father. Even though he never hurt me physically, the mental torment I went through affected my physical health as much as my social and cognitive development at the time.

According to a 2014 study by the American Psychological Association (APA), children who are emotionally, also known as psychologically, abused face similar and sometimes *worse* mental health problems as children who are physically or sexually abused. Yet, verbal torment is rarely addressed in prevention programs or in treating victims. Among the three types of abuse—emotional, physical, and sexual—emotional maltreatment was most strongly associated with depression, along with both general and social anxiety disorders in children.

Although I haven't experienced major depression that I am aware of, people close to me could tell the difference in my personality during this phase in my life. I long hesitated to write this chapter because of the sensitivity and vulnerability these personal stories entail. However, performing standup comedy has taught me being open and to some extent exposed about one's own problems and traumas has true healing powers.

Let me circle back and explain to you what led to the decision of sixteen-year-old me to leave my father. My parents got divorced when I was eleven. Even though it was a tough change for me not having both of my parents together in our home anymore, I wouldn't necessarily say I suffered from the event itself but instead suffered from what would come after.

I am an only child and a mama's boy. I always will be. There was no question about it that I would move with my mom after the divorce. Yet, three years after living with her, while seeing my dad on the weekends, I started to think about moving back in with him. At the time, it was easy for him to persuade me. He would give me cool presents, let me invite friends over, stay up late to play video games, and eat fast food whenever I wanted to. Little did I know it was going to be a living hell and an environment no kid should be living in.

The poor conditions weren't physical in nature. I had a roof over my head. The house was fine. It was the psychological mind games my dad would play on me as a young teenager trying to set me against my own mother. My mom was devastated by my decision to move. But as the great mother she is, she would let me go as she always wanted me to be happy. From that moment, destiny took its merciless course.

My mom met an amazing man who eventually became not only my stepfather but my role model who supported me and still does. My dad however would constantly have multiple women whose names I can't even remember anymore. The illusion of the fun, cool father I thought I had slowly faded away. At the time, I didn't understand what was going on.

Looking back, I realized how he gradually negatively influenced and brainwashed me. Even though I would only see my mom once a week, he started asking me why I would want to see her at all.

"Don't you think it's enough to see her only once or twice a month?"

"What has she ever done for you except giving birth? She was just an incubator for you. That's all she did."

"You could just walk up to a random woman on the street and ask her to be your mom and she would be better."

"Who do you like better? Me or your mother? You better think twice what you say now."

These were the questions I had to go through with a constant fear of giving the wrong answers that would result in him yelling at me. It was also not uncommon that plates would be thrown against the wall during dinner if I said something about my mother or tried to argue.

His choleric behavior truly intimidated me and altered my personality for the worse. My grades started suffering. I hung out with the wrong people and would always feel tension and cramping whenever I was with my mother. It wasn't because I didn't enjoy spending time with her and her new husband. Quite the contrary, I appreciated every second I could spend with them. However, I was anxious about spending too much time with her that my dad would get upset about it, which could end in whatever punishment. I didn't enjoy Christmas anymore the way a young teenager should. I turned into a melancholic, anxious kid who was fully obedient to my dad out of fear.

SCARY RELIEF
To this day, I can't really tell what finally triggered me to make a move and leave him or if it was a culmination of all the things he said and did. Yet, I eventually took a leap of faith, mustered all my courage, and was ready to go. I had enough and knew I needed to change something about my situation.

It was the first day of school after fall break in 2008. I clearly remember as though it was yesterday. I told my mom about my plan and that today would be the day. What seemed to be just another Monday where my father would drop me off at school on his way to work was the time for me to pull the trigger and escape. It was a scary relief.

School was over, and my mom and stepfather picked me up. I was crying because I was so happy to flee a situation I wouldn't have endured for one more day, and also because I was still scared of my father and the potential consequences of my actions.

The only person close to my father I told about my decision that day was his oldest friend who was also his personal assistant for many years. I always had a close and trusting relationship with her growing up.

However, that day, I told her I needed to go without a lot of explanation. I said I couldn't live like this any longer and I would be moving back with my mother and her new husband for good. Baffled and confused, she said she obviously needed to tell my father about it immediately. I responded she should tell him whatever she thought she needed to say to him, but this was my decision, and I needed her to respect it.

The following hours, I couldn't sit still. Even though I was the happiest I have ever been in a long time, I was afraid of what my father would do. Would he call me? Would he stand outside the door? Would he try to catch me at school the next day?

What really happened, though, might surprise you as much as it did me. Nothing. There was no single call, letter, email, or any other attempt to reach out or see me. To this day, he hasn't called me once, neither for Christmas nor my birthday. And I can't thank him enough for that. My decision to leave this man in my past was probably the most critical and path-breaking decision in my life. I performed better in school, I made more meaningful friends, and I started to become the fun, goofy, kind of extroverted guy I am today.

> *"We all have this trauma. The point is to transform that into being an artist, telling stories. We all have these kinds of fucked-up things that happen to us, and we can get through them. We can get through it, and transform it, and use it."*
>
> —Rainn Wilson (Comedians Tackling Depression, 2019)

I can't tell if that relationship can be considered trauma. The important thing, though, is I found a way through it. I can see it as something that changed my life for the better. It is something I am so confident about that I can easily share it with others while still being vulnerable. Rainn Wilson, comedian and actor best known for his role as Dwight Schrute on the NBC sitcom "The Office," leveraged his trauma to master his craft and become the best comedian he can possibly be:

> *"Maybe it's 'cause I was such an insecure, broke little creature that I needed that laughter to feel good about myself, but it did get me high, and I loved it."*
>
> —RAINN WILSON (COMEDIANS TACKLING DEPRESSION, 2019)

Wilson was abandoned by his mother when he was two years old and grew up with his father and stepmother. In those early years in our lives, when we need our mother's love the most, being separated from her and breaking this unique bond can have some profound effects on our personalities. He would not see her again until he was fifteen, which left a mark on him that changed his life forever. However, what started out as being an insecure, odd, ungainly boy turned into a man known for being the funniest in the room, and someone people would want to be around.

Wilson didn't let his inner wounds erode him. Instead, he converted and reconstructed them and used them for something good, which eventually helped him survive. Through performing comedy and being an artist, he found a way to tell his story. He was able to cope with his past by facing it in the present moment.

During the summit event in January 2019, Ray Dalio, hedge fund manager and philanthropist, perfectly summarized it by saying, "Pain plus reflection equals progress." Rainn Wilson used his pain to his advantage, confronted while reflected on his pain, and created something beautiful.

EMBRACING FAILURE BRINGS HEALTH
I can't stress enough how crucial it is to train your mental muscles and take care of your psychological health as much as you would your physical well-being. Beyond that, seeking professional help in times of hardship is not any more unusual than seeing a doctor when you have the flu or stomach pain. Yet, it is also important to mention that a poor mental condition can have negative impacts on our physical state as much as low physical health can lead to an increased risk of developing psychiatric disorders.

It was during my time in college in Germany when I first contemplated seeing a therapist. As I'm writing this, I am curious to see how many friends will reach out to me after reading my story to tell me they didn't have a single clue about what was going on with me back then.

I was never a good student. I was the kind who had to study ten times as hard as my classmates to pass my exam. But as you might imagine, studying ten times longer than your friends didn't work out all the time and wasn't sustainable. If there had been an award for most failed classes within an academic year, I would have easily won it. I am not exaggerating when I say there were semesters in which I didn't pass a single exam.

I studied economics at a renowned university in Cologne, Germany, because this is what you had to do: majoring in economics or business administration to eventually end up working as a consultant or investment banker. Pursuing something creative or doing anything other than going to college was regarded as odd by others.

Although technically it was my sophomore year, I had at least two more ahead of me to graduate because I had failed so many classes. It was pure mental torture. Seeing your friends around you slowly start to graduate and get jobs while I was still struggling to pass classes from freshman year made me question everything. I was on the brink of dropping out. So, then what? I would be a total disappointment for my parents, I thought. In my mind, I thought my family would be ashamed of talking about me because of my poor academic performance.

It seemed like my life collapsed like a house of cards. I didn't enjoy going out with my friends anymore or spending time with my girlfriend. I was scared. It wouldn't be uncommon that I cried at my parents' dinner table because of the fear of being a letdown to them and my friends. I broke up with my girlfriend because I was mentally drained and overwhelmed. I kept finding other reasons and excuses to end our relationship, hurting her even more instead of just telling the truth. But I wasn't able to tell her what was going on inside of me. It felt like a battle I had to fight within myself that nobody else could help me with.

I did not open up more about this issue because I thought my problems were not "bad" enough to be real problems. I knew friends and family members who had much more adversity to deal with. Who was I to complain about college problems and feeling mentally overwhelmed?

> *No matter what hardships we are going through, there is always a moment we consider rock bottom, and it can only get better from there.*
>
> —FELIX DEY

What my rock bottom back then looked like might be a big surprise for people who know me, but I feel it is essential to talk about it. My college campus was not too far away from my hometown. In fact, I would drive every day for fifty miles (eighty kilometers) back and forth to get to classes. When taking the freeway, or what we call *Autobahn* in Germany, I occasionally thought about what would happen if I would just speed up, crash my car on purpose and die. It wasn't that I actively thought about dying by suicide, but just imagining the process and how people would remember and think of me was liberating and relieving to me.

Let me quickly explain why I explicitly chose to say "dying by" and not "committing suicide" as it plays a crucial role in fighting the overall stigma still attached to it. The word "commit" has a negative meaning associated with it as it is also used when saying, for example, "committing adultery" or "committing murder." The phrase "committing suicide" is misleading because it goes back to an era when suicide was considered a sin or a crime. For example, in the UK, it wasn't until the English Suicide Act in 1961 that suicide would no longer be deemed criminal. (Suicide Act, 1961)

Sadly enough, still today, suicide is a crime in some parts of the world. Section 309 of the East Indian Penal Code states, "Whoever attempts to commit suicide and does any act toward the commission of such offence, shall be punished with simple imprisonment for a term which may extend to one year or with fine, or with both." Although this legislation was restricted by the East Indian Mental Health Act in 2017, suicide is still frowned upon in Indian society.

Susan Beaton, a suicide prevention adviser who explored mental health terminology in her research report "Suicide and Language: Why We Shouldn't Use the 'C' Word," said, "We now live in a time when we seek to understand people who experience suicidal ideation, behaviors, and attempts, and to treat them with compassion rather than condemn them. Part of this is to use appropriate, non-stigmatizing terminology when referring to suicide."

"Suicidal ideations are a pressure release valve," said Bill Bernat in his TED talk "How to Connect with Depressed Friends." Looking back, I understand how the mental visualization of crashing my car and dying was a way of feeling emotionally liberated from the anguish I was trapped in.

It allowed me to zoom out and forget about the struggles I was going through for a moment. I asked myself what my friends and family would say at my funeral. Who would even show up? Would my father come? What photos and videos from me are they going to show? Thinking about these scenarios gave me this odd feeling of appreciation and external validation that I do matter. It showed me that my friends and family love me regardless of how good or bad I am performing in college or anywhere else.

It was also during this time when I first started to think about seeing a therapist. I just had this strong inner desire to talk to someone who would be totally unbiased, someone who is neither my best friend, my girlfriend, nor my parents. I just needed someone to pour my heart out to, someone who wouldn't listen or respond, but would instead understand and empathize.

The only person I talked about this with was one of my close friends who sees a therapist herself. However, finding professional help turned out to be a difficult task. Eventually, I did not see a therapist. Not because I decided against it, but because the supply for professional mental health heavily outweighs the demand and would have put me on a waiting list for at least six months. Fortunately, though, my situation improved. I can't tell you exactly what the pivotal moment was that brought me out of my inner misery. It wasn't necessarily one moment or one conversation I had, but a culmination of good things over a period of time.

My mother and stepfather supported me throughout, and after a lot of sweat, blood, and tears, I managed to do better in college and take care of my mental health. I enjoyed being out with friends again and even got back together with my girlfriend.

I am telling you all of this to let you know every story has its unique characteristics somebody can relate to. What might not be worth sharing or talking about for you, because it's not a "bad or good enough" story, may help others because they're going through something similar.

I made a mistake to think I wasn't in the position to open up about what I was dealing with and what was occupying my mind. I felt like a phony with my problems. Was I "officially" depressed at the time? I cannot tell you that. But was I feeling anxious and like everything would start falling apart? Absolutely. Fortunately, I found my way through it with the help of loved ones. It doesn't always need to be a massive trauma, family tragedy, or genetic condition to feel miserable and anxious. Although depression has many faces, one thing is fair to say: They are never pretty.

CORE LESSONS

- Emotionally abused children face similar and sometimes *worse* mental health problems as children who are physically or sexually abused.

- Openness and vulnerability enable true healing powers.

- Pain + reflection = progress.

- There is an important distinction between committing suicide and dying by suicide.

- Suicidal ideations are an emotional pressure release valve that help keep mental pain in check. Don't be afraid or ashamed of them but share them with a loved one.

PART 2

THE WEIRDO IN THE ROOM

CHAPTER 4

THE HISTORY OF COMEDY

"You see, a comedian, by the very nature of what he is, is a troublemaker. He is an iconoclast. He is a playful troublemaker, a good-natured troublemaker, but a troublemaker, and therefore he must recognize the existence of certain taboos."

—Steve Allen

I want you to take a moment and think about what happens when you meet someone for the first time, whether it is at your new job, on a date, or at your neighbor's party. How do these conversations usually start? You begin by asking each other a series of questions such as:

- Where did you grow up?
- How did you guys get to know each other?
- How long have you been living here?

The importance of history in defining just about any subject cannot be emphasized enough. Everything begins with a chat about an individual or collective past event, whether you are switching to a new occupation, seeing a doctor, or catching up with your friends.

The same is true for the history of comedy. To fully understand the importance standup comedy has on just about any topic today, we must have a sound knowledge of where it came from and what a comedian's initial motivation was that could change a society's perspective and even disrupt entire regimes.

We can make sense of where we are nowadays and how we got here by examining comedy's origins. It helps to set a stage upon which its story can be told. The high art of farce, at least as we know it today, has not been around for too long. Unlike its big brothers and sisters, theatre, music, and poetry, which can be traced back thousands of years, standup is a fairly recent form of entertainment.

Its beginnings can be found between the late 1800s and early 1900s. But like any form of (live) entertainment today, comedy went through decades of evolution and progress. Having someone perform on stage, talking to hundreds or thousands of people about highly controversial social issues or their own neuroses and foibles was unheard of and could even lead to severe punishments for the entertainer.

THE BEGINNINGS: FROM CLEAN TO NOT SO CLEAN
Originated in France at the end of the nineteenth century, Vaudeville was live entertainment consisting of various individual performances such as singers, dancers, acrobats,

magicians, and occasionally comedians. During that time in the early 1900s, comedy became an industry in the US for the first time. It was used to perform "clean" humor to a broad audience. Comedians were supposed to stay away from any topics considered controversial. The obedient and compliant comics were widely preferred by the general public over their vulgar counterparts.

In fact, "Clean Bills" became a famous phrase in the entertainment industry, which referred to performances where high quality, immaculate humor was guaranteed. These were the kind of shows large crowds would attend and appreciate a wide variety of entertainment without the vulgarity. If, however, a Vaudevillian performed something on stage that was objectionable, a blue envelope was sent backstage with the material the makers of the show wanted excised from the comedian's act. This phrase has prevailed with modern standup comedy to this day when we talk about "blue material" in a performance, which is seen as shocking. Today, the only difference is that nobody forces comedians to cut out that material or checks your work before a live show anymore, at least if it isn't being recorded for commercial television.

What we consider offensive though, evolves with every generation. Like Patton Oswalt, a famous American comedian and actor would say in the CNN show "The History of Comedy," "Off-limits is not a permanent address. It's just a marker that keeps getting moved."

In the early 1900s, the whole family would watch live, clean theatrical entertainment on a Saturday night. Burlesque shows made a name for themselves by offering something different. It is no secret that a Burlesque audience, which consisted mostly of men, enjoyed this kind of entertainment because of the scantily clad ladies. However, comedians were regular performers at these shows, too. The only problem they were faced with, though, was that they had to do something that would upstage a naked woman to attract attention, which resulted in performing a sort of dirty humor. Eventually, comedians were appreciated by the audience for their more shocking and obscene materials.

SPEAKING TRUTH TO POWER

Many names in comedy are worth mentioning that contributed richly to what it is today. Their stories are diverse and intriguing, but when talking about the history of comedy, one cannot overlook Lenny Bruce and Richard Pryor. Although they're from two different generations, both paved the way.

> *"I'm not a comedian. And I'm not sick. The world is sick, and I'm the doctor. I'm a surgeon with a scalpel for false values."*
>
> —LENNY BRUCE (THE HISTORY OF COMEDY, 2017)

Lenny Bruce was the first of his kind who openly and in an entertaining manner addressed and criticized social and political issues during the 1950s and early 1960s. In an effort to impose the right of freedom of speech, both on and off stage, Bruce was repeatedly hounded and pilloried for profanity by speaking in a way most people today would regard as normal and even good natured.

He broke down the walls to clear the way for new openness for thousands of comedians to come after him. Bruce was not only an entertainer but a social critic, challenging our language, pushing the boundaries, and taking the hit for all of us performers. It made him a target for his skeptics and law enforcement, leading to an infamous 1964 arrest on stage in New York City. He was eventually convicted of obscenity and was sentenced to four months in a workhouse but remained out on bail. Yet, following his verdict, he hardly found a stage to perform on again. By 1966, Bruce had been blacklisted by almost every nightclub in the United States, as club owners feared prosecution, making him virtually unemployable.

In the early 1970s, vaudeville and burlesque finally came together at the Friars Club, a private association in New York City that would host televised roasts, starting with "The Dean Martin Celebrity Roast." It was a show in which Dean Martin, one of the most famous entertainers, and fellow comics, playfully embarrassed a famous icon publicly in an always hilarious fashion. For the first time, individuals were publicly insulted and made fun of for the sake of comedy and entertainment. Blue material was still present, but it didn't have the same strict limitations and restrictions it had decades before.

LET'S GET PERSONAL

During this time, Pryor began performing in front of large crowds in the early 1960s, when standup comedy itself experienced a significant change. Routines became more personal. Experimenting with standup as a form of intimate expression was a trend that started back then and has stuck around ever since. In fact, many comedians come from troubled circumstances. Consequently, their image as those damaged and troubled people in our society who are funny has become a common perception throughout the years.

For almost a century, comedians have been agents of social action and change. They have challenged cultural assumptions, stereotypes, and stigma. Richard Pryor, who had his comedic breakthrough in 1973 by winning his first Emmy (best writing in comedy, variety), pioneered a brand of visceral comedy. Still, he needed Lenny Bruce to suffer before him to make space and create greater acceptance for his comedic style. Pryor made profanity seem to be part of everyday life. He changed low comedy into high art, keeping his authenticity while speaking truth to power politically and consciously. Because of Pryor, there were fewer barriers to break through for every new standup comedian. Consequently, they would reach further and try to do something that would shock the audience.

> "You either laugh through it
> or you die through it."
>
> —RAIN PRYOR (THE HISTORY OF COMEDY, 2017)

Rain Pryor is Richard's daughter. She beautifully summarized how her father endured a miserable childhood and adolescence but catalyzed it to become one of the most influential standup comedians of all time. His mother was a prostitute in a brothel run by his grandmother in growing Peoria, Illinois.

On a daily basis, he would see various random men enter his home, which was the brothel, and disappear with his mother into the bedroom. Troubled with her own problems, Pryor's mother left him with his abusive grandmother when he was ten. He was facing two options: succumb to his external world or pour it into his comedic talents.

As history showed, luckily, he chose the latter. I can't even imagine how many people in our world today live under similar circumstances and are forced to choose between dying through it or using their talents, whatever those might be, to find a way out. Obviously, this is easier said than done, and not everybody is blessed with a particular gift.

In my comedy school's classes, I could literally see the pain so many of my fellow classmates went and still go through. Although they would just use words, I was able to put myself into their positions. It was scary yet beautiful to see how lightheartedly they opened up about personal setbacks and tragedies.

I remember my classmate Nora on stage making fun of herself and her last relationship. Nothing unusual so far as you would think. Tragically enough, Nora endured a physically abusive relationship that would leave a deep scar not only on her body, but also on her mind. For way too long, she couldn't end a relationship that was constantly leaving her with bruises, broken bones, and black eyes. Yet, the courage she had to address that openly in front of people she barely knew created a special energy and atmosphere in the room I have carried with me ever since.

For many of us, including myself, her experiences and way of dealing with them on a comedic stage showed that our lives' darkest chapters can be turned around into a source of creativity and power. I could feel her sorrow yet relief when she spoke about her past relationship because I myself had been abused by someone I considered a loved one for too many years. Even though he never laid a hand on me, my father hurt me emotionally when I was a child.

I immediately sensed this special bond between Nora and me, even though we never exchanged a word until this point. For the first time, I realized standup is strongly rooted in empathy, making space for the unexpressed and unspoken. Nora decided not to give in to the emotional and physical pain her ex-boyfriend left her with, but to share and use it. Instead of trying to bury her misery, she processed and eventually overcame it, one punchline at a time.

As bad and ugly as Richard Pryor's early life was, it contributed to the man, standup comedian, actor, and writer he eventually became. Pryor's comedy was the steppingstone for others to open up and be hilariously vulnerable and brutally honest about their lives. It was the first time standup comedians used their stages the way therapists use their couches.

WOMEN ARE HERE TO STAY

In the history of comedy, female standup artists had to fight a long battle filled with sexism and biases alleging that it's not in women's nature to be funny, and they still do. However, society came a long way from systematically discriminating against women to female comics selling out entire football stadiums. Yet, the path toward today's standards, which are still far from perfect, has been a rocky but revolutionary one.

Humor is a powerful social tool that any person, if applied correctly, can use to their advantage to convey an important message to the masses. Ever since women stepped into the comedic arena and began to harness their humorous energies, there have always been individuals, if not entire societies, who would want them to fail and vanish into thin air. The question was not if women were and are funny, but if the community they are in lets them be funny.

Being a comedian means giving one's opinion to a diverse audience. Today it is absurd to imagine a comedy world without female contributions. Women are influential in the world of standup because of not only their anatomies, but also their life experiences, which are entirely different from that of men. Hence there is that much more to mine for comedic material to present to an audience.

In the early 1900s, a woman on stage expressing her opinion in front of men was not really accepted. It's been perceived as threatening in the same way that a woman getting an education once was. As a lady, being attractive *and* funny at the same time was unheard of. Not even parents wanted their daughters to be hilarious or entertaining. How would a funny woman ever get married if she posed a risk for the man's ego and dignity?

At the beginning of the twentieth century, women's only chance to stand out on stage was as slapstick sidekicks in silent comedy. When Vaudeville came along, it allowed them to shine as singers or dancers. However, once their male counterparts hit the stage, they sadly became just a part of the scenery, handling props or supervising scripts.

Jean Carroll broke through this wall and became one of the first accepted female comedians. She was married to another comic, Buddy Howe, with whom she would do comedy. After Buddy eventually went off to war, she rewrote their act and did it by herself, playing huge venues in the late 1940s.

Phyllis Diller followed Carroll's footsteps as she entered the predominant male standup arena in the 1950s and switched the sexist point of view; instead of talking about a horrible wife or mother-in-law, she talked about a terrible husband. These brave women finally gave female audience members something to relate to.

As much as humor fuels a man's life, it certainly drives that of a woman too. A female-deprived comedy world would be a sad and dull one. As lead character Miriam Maisel in the top-rated television series "The Marvelous Mrs. Maisel" says:

> *"Comedy is fueled by oppression, by the lack of power, by sadness and disappointment, by abandonment, and humiliation. Now, who the hell does that describe more than women? Judging by those standards, only women should be funny."*

It is obviously no secret that, first and foremost, comedy's role is to be entertaining. The majority of comics out there aren't here to change the world. However, as history shows, standup has a number of positive by-products. These can include subverting society's norms or helping an individual coping with mental or physical hardships.

Out of my personal experience, making people laugh has the potential to make us feel better, whatever state we're in. And if they (the audience) are laughing, it usually means they're listening. Being heard or listened to creates an intimate, informal space in which we can deal with complex and painful subjects.

Humor is intertwined with our everyday existence. It allows us to articulate complicated emotions and issues by using jokes as a framing mechanism. There is something about the immediacy of comedy that will enable us to speak honestly and openly about even the most hurtful things.

However dark the material, there's always a humorous angle. Performing standup can still be a scary and intimidating experience. But the benefits of doing it clearly outweigh the risks that we might associate with it, such as embarrassment and shame. When we're laughing at ourselves, we consciously run rings around ourselves. Still, we're also the ones taking the superior attitude. Even when we're still suffering, we can find a point of view from which our misery is not the most serious thing about ourselves anymore.

CORE LESSONS
- Comedians have always been agents of social action and change. They have challenged social assumptions, stereotypes, and stigma.

- Comedy pushes boundaries and comments on society and the world we're living in.

- If you can make them laugh, you will make them listen.

- Humor is a form of psychological processing.

- When you can laugh at yourself or about your adversity, your suffering is not the most serious thing about you anymore.

CHAPTER 5

FEELING HOMESICK AT HOME

"I think all of us romanticize depression to a degree, but I'd rather be well. There's nothing more important to me than being funny, except being well."

—SARAH SILVERMAN

The two-time Emmy Award-winning comedian Sarah Silverman has done it all. At age twenty-three, she started as a writer for Saturday Night Live, made her network standup comedy debut on the "Late Show with David Letterman" at twenty-six, and has quickly risen to one of today's funniest comedians. She had her own show on Comedy Central for three years, published a memoir, and released her Netflix standup special "Sarah Silverman: A Speck of Dust," which scored a 100 percent on Rotten Tomatoes.

Sarah is an inspiration for many young people not only in comedy but also in the arts in general. However, being in comedy comes with a lot of negativity and self-deprecation. As with many other success stories, Sarah's story is marked by fights. These battles are usually against critics, naysayers, and fellow comedians. But the biggest of them all is the clash against herself and her depression. Even long before she made her first steps on a comedy club stage, she started the fight against this malicious mental condition.

Growing up as the youngest of four girls in a middle-class Jewish family in Manchester, New Hampshire, Sarah was always the class clown among her family and friends. She understood pretty early in her life that she was born with a specific skill set, which was being funny. Precisely these capabilities allowed her to distract others from the physical appearance she was so ashamed about. She was this "tiny kid covered in black hair with big teeth that didn't fit her little head," as she would say.

Sarah first experienced depression when she was thirteen after she came home from a school camping trip. There wasn't a triggering moment during this school trip that made her depressed from one moment to another. Instead, it was a cumulation of insecurity, self-doubt, and shame. She was a bed wetter and when in school, would carry Pampers hidden in her sleeping bag—a huge and shameful secret to carry for any young teenager.

Even at this young age, Sarah quickly realized something was off. Soon after that trip, she went from being the class clown to not seeing life in that casual and easy way anymore. She couldn't deal with being around her friends anymore and didn't go to school for months at a time as she started having panic attacks.

Her parents, who were already divorced at the time and remarried others, did the best they could to help by sending her to therapists. With all the loving support she received from her family, everyone around her tried to find ways to help her without really knowing what depression actually felt like.

Even though there are common symptoms of depression and anxiety, it is as individual and unique as it can get. Affected people can experience feelings of sadness, emptiness, or hopelessness. Others may never feel unusually sad but have angry outbursts, irritability, or frustration, even over small matters against their closest friends and family.

Multiple studies have also shown that particularly young men and women in their twenties who have depression symptoms were more likely than their non-depressed peers to engage in high-risk sexual behavior. Feelings of worthlessness and the desire for social validation could become a catalyst to a more active sexual lifestyle and more irresponsible sexual behavior.

One day, though, Sarah's stepfather asked her what it actually feels like for her.

> *"It feels like I'm desperately homesick, but I'm home."*
>
> —SARAH SILVERMAN

As her mental state wouldn't become any better and she started to experience severe panic attacks, Sarah was put on Xanax, a prescription medicine used to treat anxiety disorders and depression. "They would just up the dose and up the dose and up the dose," Sarah said, up to the point where she took four Xanax four times a day.

As young as thirteen, Sarah went to see her first therapist. At the time, sending her to therapy and getting her the medication she required was the only way her parents could help her. Ironically and tragically enough, Sarah's first therapist died by suicide after hanging himself. From there on, she went on a long journey of seeing several therapists and taking her daily dose of sixteen Xanax in her teenage years.

It is no secret the heavy use of a benzodiazepine medication such as Xanax can lead to addiction, overdose, and death. Feeling the addiction slowly becoming more present in Sarah's life, a few years later, her mother took her to a new psychiatrist who got her completely off medication within six months. It was that last half pill she took at the high school water fountain when she was sixteen and realized she was ready to live a mentally healthy life again without any drugs.

Sarah made it! She won the fight against herself. A fight that was loud, fierce, rugged, and seemingly unending from the inside. From the outside, people had a hard time understanding what was going on. Nothing is subtler or more elusive than our minds and our emotions.

For the next six years, Sarah lived a life full of joy, fun, and curiosity, and, most importantly, without any medication. It was during that time when she made her first step on the comedy stage at the Boston Comedy Club in Greenwich Village. Even though she described her first standup show as awful, her passion for comedy and making other people laugh had gripped her already.

Eventually, she went to New York University (NYU) to study drama and began distributing flyers for New York City comedy clubs in exchange for five-minute spots. Her academic career wouldn't last long, though. Her passion, talent, and enthusiasm for comedy and a life in the arts would quickly be more enticing than the insides of a lecture hall.

After dropping out of NYU, she was hired as a writer-performer for "Saturday Night Live." Quickly after, a role in the HBO sketch comedy series "Mr. Show" followed, and she made her network standup comedy debut on "The Late Show with David Letterman"—a dream of every comedian out there who wants to end up on the big stages. Everything seemed in tune.

DEPRESSION, A FREQUENT VISITOR

> *"It happened as fast as the sun going behind a cloud."*
>
> —SARAH SILVERMAN

Sarah's dark phase during her teenage years filled with self-doubt, anxiety, listlessness, and panic attacks was fortunately defeated and forgotten. It was a regular night in her New York City apartment. She was letting the evening come to an end watching an episode of "90210" when all of a sudden, it came over her again. She knew the feeling immediately: depression. Panic. Anxiety. She thought it was gone forever. But it was back.

Just as cancer, depression is a highly recurrent disease that can put a person right back into this fatal dark place they once fought so bravely to escape it. According to Dr. William Marchand, a clinical associate professor of psychiatry at the University of Utah School of Medicine, the risk of recurrence—relapse after full remission—for a person who's had one episode of depression is 50 percent. This usually happens within five years.

However, it can occur weeks, months, or even many years after going through the first episode. Moreover, for a person with two episodes, the risk is about 70 percent. For someone with three episodes or more, the risk rises to around 90 percent.

The chance that symptoms will return is prevalent and real. They might get better at times and get worse at others, but it doesn't ever feel like depression is gone. Just because someone recovered from a torn Achilles tendon doesn't mean this person wouldn't suffer another similar injury in the future. The same goes for mental health conditions like depression.

However, we can strengthen our physical muscles to make them stronger and prevent another injury from happening. Just as our hamstrings and calves are muscles we can train, our brain is a muscle, too—the most powerful one. Anyone who went through a muscle injury and rehab knows how much time, patience, and will power it takes to come back from it. Usually, the worse the injury is, the harder its recovery will be. Recovering from depression and preventing it from happening again requires exactly that effort and patience and must not be taken lightly.

Filled with fear of being trapped in this vicious cycle again, she called her friend who would immediately send her to a psychiatrist at two in the morning that same night. As happy as she was living a life without medication for the last decade, she was happy her new psychiatrist put her on *Klonopin*, an anti-epileptic drug used to treat panic attacks.

Initially plagued by doubts about whether she could defeat her inner demons again, Sarah found a healthy way of living with depression and learned to control it. Even though she sometimes experienced those same symptoms she had when she was younger, there's one thing she knows now that she didn't back then: It will pass. And it did. She found her light at the end of the tunnel.

As much as being funny is and always will be a considerable part of her life, she realized dealing with mental health conditions will remain throughout. The difference though is that with depression, we just have to be brave enough to exist through it.

> I've lived with depression and learned to control it, or at least to ride the waves as best I can. My medication, combined with therapy, keeps me healthy but still lets me feel highs and lows. The dark years and those ups and downs—chemical and otherwise—have always informed my work; I believe being a comedian is about exposing yourself, warts and all.
>
> —Sarah Silverman

(NO LONGER) SUFFERING IN SILENCE

Being honest about our feelings and emotions is never an easy step. It takes a lot of courage and inner strength to open up about even positive emotions. I remember myself struggling for weeks, if not months, to tell my then-girlfriend for the first time that I loved her. I pictured different scenarios of how she would respond. These so-called "what-if" scenarios went through my head over and over again.

- What if she doesn't feel the same way?

- What if it's too early to tell her?

- What if it's already too late and she thinks I'm not emotionally invested in our relationship even though I would move mountains for her?

The reason we sometimes feel so insecure talking about our emotions is that we make ourselves vulnerable. It is like being alone on stage, revealing our deepest secrets, and explicitly asking to get judged by whomever is watching.

In most cases, it's our friends and family, sometimes co-workers in that audience judging us. When it comes to mental health problems, accepting and admitting we are struggling is an important step toward recovery. It is where all healing begins, yet it is so hard to get to it in the first place.

> *"Those secrets kill. That the secret of keeping all that to yourself and putting on that mask—that'll eat away at you daily and ate away at me daily."*
>
> —WAYNE BRADY

Talking about problems of any kind is challenging. However, it becomes even harder if your personal and professional life is on the line. This is both a blessing and curse for people in the limelight. Once you reach a certain level of popularity and fame, you sacrifice pieces of your personal life being exposed to the public.

For comedians in particular, whose job it is to be "the funny one," this becomes a double burden. Just like Sarah Silverman, Wayne Brady is one of those comics who gained fame and success through his comedic talents. Also known as a TV star of shows like "Whose Line Is It Anyway?" and "Let's Make a Deal," Brady rose to fame with his squeaky-clean yet hilarious persona.

What most people didn't know, even the ones closest to him, is that this same persona was infested with a parasite for many years. An unwanted passenger that left him in despair and threw him into a cruel spiral of self-doubt. Plagued with fear of coming out or being exposed, he secretly battled with depression for years.

> "Having a bad day is one thing, having a bad week or a bad life is another. You don't want to move; you can't move in the darkness. You're like, 'I am just going to sit right here, and I want to wallow in this. As much

as it hurts, I am going to sit right here because this is what I deserve. This is what I deserve, so I am going to sit here because I am that horrible of a person.'"

—Wayne Brady

For many people, traveling all around the country and being on stage in front of thousands of people, like Brady did and still does, is the ultimate goal. From the outside, it seems like these people lack nothing. They are getting admired by their fans and community, invited to the most prestigious hotels and restaurants around the globe, and can make a living out of their passion. That is what Hollywood can do for you. Within a heartbeat, the entertainment industry can carry you toward money and fame, making you forget all the hard times you may have faced in your past.

However, there is a different side to it, too. A side only very few are brave enough to talk about. There's a lingering bitterness inside Hollywood's breeding grounds. We all know headlines of yet another famous actor, singer, songwriter battling alcohol or drug addiction. Seeing someone from the industry going into rehab is nothing that shocks us anymore—and it's nothing the show business makes a scene about.

According to Brady, outing yourself among fellow entertainers to be an alcoholic or drug addict is actually considered cool by some. The image that you aren't a real rockstar or Hollywood actor if you haven't been to rehab at least once is one yet too present and accurate. Opening up about being clinically depressed, having mental breakdowns, or just feeling unhappy, though, is viewed as fake and doesn't get much if any attention. Yet, empathy and connection are precisely what these people who are suffering need.

HOW CINEMA STIGMATIZES MENTAL ILLNESS

Hollywood's stigma attached to mental health found its beginnings in the early years of film making and is still present to this day. It is not only that popular movies and TV shows hardly portray mental health conditions, but if they do, the characters are often shown being violent or treated disparagingly.

A 2019 report by the USC Annenberg Inclusion Initiative reveals that 46 percent of film characters and 25 percent of TV characters with a mental health condition demonstrate violent or aggressive behavior. This depiction is simply not accurate and far from reality, mental health experts around the world argue.

Moreover, language does play an essential role in increasing or reducing stigma, as well. Words and phrases such as *psycho, creep, sociopath, unstable, and ruined* are no stranger in movies and TV shows showing characters struggling with mental health conditions. Over time, these images triggered an adverse effect that has hurt the perception of people struggling with this in the real world.

The very first horror movies that appeared in the 1960s, such as *Psycho* by Alfred Hitchcock, nurtured the continuing confusion about the relationship between schizophrenia and dissociative identity disorder. Even supernatural films like *The Exorcist* (1973) promote the idea that mental illness is the equivalent of possession by the devil.

However, we have seen progress toward broader, sensitive portrayals of mental illness in the twenty-first century through movies such as *Silver Linings Playbook* (2012). In this star-studded blockbuster, mental illness is not shown as some moral or spiritual shortcoming but highlights the relevance of mental health treatment. Yet, the portrayal of the killing clown, possessed nanny, or sociopathic neighbor remains as Hollywood still tends to swing occasionally from sentimentality to sensationalism.

The most recent example is Joaquin Phoenix as Arthur Fleck in *Joker* (2019), a failed standup comic who turns into a psychopath with a warped, sadistic sense of humor. But please don't get me wrong. In fact, I must admit that *Joker* was one of the best movies I saw in 2019. It's not surprising that it won not one but two Oscars.

The movie's underlying message wasn't to glorify yet another individual struggling with mental illness, which goes on a killing spree. Instead, it attempts to shine a light on society's controversial topics in which "the other guy" gets ignored and left behind by the wealthy and prosperous.

Comedy, though, was what helped Brady to get this parasite out of his body and mind.

> *"Just being good at this and trying to be funny and trying to be smart and trying to get the laugh, that's the thing that I was able to use to self-soothe."*

Depression is something that's part of the human condition. Yet, it still remains challenging and complicated for people to accept, support, and talk about. I understand it is not a condition easy to comprehend and to make sense of as its symptoms can have so many diverse faces. Yet, reading about these comedians and understanding how they grasp a disease that is so hard to put into words enhanced my overall perspective about it and even helped me better cope with tragedy.

It gave me a nudge toward becoming more self-aware while being more compassionate with others—regardless of their background, current circumstances, or medical condition. Beyond that, it also shows us that mental health treatments are as unique as its problems and people find ever more creative ways to battle their inner demons. No longer are treatment options either extreme (electroconvulsive therapy) or overly stereotyped and simplistic (therapists' couch sessions).

For me, I found going on walks or hikes while listening to podcasts relaxing. It allows me to decompress my mind, mostly at the end of the day, and go within. Other options include meditation, physical activities, and interventions by family and friends to medication management, group sessions, or prayer. *You* alone will figure out what works best for *you*. There is nothing more uplifting than recognizing what does and doesn't work for you. Do the inner work, and the results will follow. I promise you that!

CORE LESSONS

- Depression and anxiety can affect people in various ways. From feelings of sadness, emptiness, or hopelessness to never feeling unusually sad but having angry outbursts, irritability, or frustration.

- The risk of recurrence—relapse after full remission—for a person who's had one episode of depression is 50 percent.

- Accepting and admitting we are struggling is an important step toward recovery. It is where all healing begins.

- Language in modern day movies and television plays a crucial role in reducing stigma.

CHAPTER 6

GO HEAL YOURSELF

―

"Comedy is not going to save you, and if you are thinking about doing comedy as a substitute for therapy, it definitely doesn't work. I tried. I tried for a long time."

—CHRIS GETHARD

For many people, humor is an effective way of dealing with personal hardships and adversity. Dr. Ramon Mora-Ripoll is an expert in mind-body therapies like therapeutic humor. His research showed how laughter has physiological, psychological, social, and spiritual benefits. Although therapeutic efficacy of laughter is mainly derived from spontaneous laughter (triggered by external stimuli or positive emotions) and self-induced laughter (triggered by oneself at will), sufficient evidence suggests laughter has some positive, quantifiable effects on certain aspects of health.

It only seems logical then that comedians use their craft as both a coping mechanism for depression and stage time as a self-prescribed therapy. Yet, after I did more research on comedians and their unique struggle with depression, I was proven otherwise when comedy veteran Chris Gethard opened up about his ongoing battle with depression and how it tied to his passion of writing and performing standup.

Growing up in an Irish American family in West Orange, New Jersey, Chris admired comedians who seemed to be able to do whatever they wanted, such as Howard Stern, Andy Kaufman, and David Letterman. This interest heavily influenced his later comedic persona to speak recklessly about controversial topics like drug abuse and suicide fantasies.

Chris first started to feel something was off in fifth grade. He began to feel aware he was not on the same wavelength as his fellow classmates. In his 2017 HBO standup comedy special "Career Suicide," he mentioned, "I didn't know when I was eleven years old that this thing had a name: depression." By ninth grade, he was deeply in his own head and already very adept at hiding how he was feeling on the inside. Like cancer would find its way through various parts of an infected body, the first signs of depression slowly crept upon him.

As Chris became older and made comedy his passion, he found a way out of the dark places he was stuck in for most of his school-age life. However, as a newbie standup comedian who was, according to his words, "depressed, fucked up, and looking for any excuse to not get help," he saw it as a justification not to talk to anyone about his agonies as his early comedy heroes were struggling with depression, too.

While attending college in New Jersey, Chris began taking classes at Manhattan's Upright Citizens Brigade Theatre (UCB), the only accredited improv and sketch comedy school in the country. At UCB, Chris quickly made a name for himself, rising in its ranks and even becoming part of the UCB Theater's national touring company. His unique style of authentically making fun of issues related to drug addiction and depression made him share the same stage with big names such as Amy Poehler, Jason Mantzoukas, or Rob Corddry. The prospects for a successful comedy career were excellent.

However, it was also during this time when the depression had taken over. During his time in college, he would have one of two dreams *every* night for a year: In one dream, Chris got into a confrontation where he throws a punch, but he would not be able to complete it, and his whole movement froze.

In another dream, the TV on his bookshelf began to fall leaving Chris in perpetual tension trying to keep the TV upright. What happened was he turned his mental level of anxiety into physical pain waking up every single morning for a year in constant pain in his neck and shoulders.

At age twenty-one, he eventually hit rock bottom. When a car cut him off on a suburban New Jersey road, he wouldn't hit the brakes, figuring this was the easiest way to end his life without bringing shame to his family. In the 2019 YouTube documentary *Comedians Tackling Depression & Anxiety Makes Us Feel Seen*, he recalls, "I wouldn't say I crashed the car on purpose, but the way I always describe it is there was an accident happening, and I kind of went with it."

Even though his mental health seemed to be on a free fall, his professional comedy career was on an upswing, a dangerously fine line to be walking. A couple of years into comedy and improv, Chris would get thousands of people excited about his unique comedic persona. It felt like his long-awaited comedy breakthrough was within his reach.

His two best friends on his improv team, Bobby Moynihan and Zach Woods, eventually got their big breaks with "Saturday Night Live" and "The Office," respectively. Chris was supposed to be next in line, patiently waiting and showing off his talent day in and day out. However, over and over, up and coming, younger standup comics passed him. All those young talents moved on to become bigger and better, or at least moved to Hollywood, the comedy capital.

His dream of becoming a big name in comedy slowly shattered as it was eclipsed by reality time and again. During this time, his depression became even worse and his material increasingly dark and melancholic, encouraged by the demon inside of him. With the little hope he thought he had left, he went on to create "The Chris Gethard Show," first as a live show at UCB and eventually on public access television. The show earned a cult following, but the sort that others in the scene viewed as overhauled and dead.

The tragic tale of a talented comedian who was once featured on Variety magazine's "Ten Comics to Watch in 2010" list but never made a move to Hollywood ran its course. Plagued with the uncertainty of how his whole life would unfold, Chris' mental state was trapped in this dark space we don't even want our greatest enemy to sojourn.

As many other depressive people would also share during my research, Chris felt it was only getting worse, and he didn't know how to stop it. Even though he was constantly surrounded by his family and closest friends, he woke up feeling not just depressed but also a profound level of isolated sadness. The more he tried to climb out of it, the worse it became.

I describe myself as a fairly approachable and communicative person. I open up to friends, even people I just met, rather quickly because I know that everyone is screwed up or broken in a certain way. Along my way of doing standup, I realize those who seem to have it together on the surface are just experts at hiding their fears and anxieties somewhere deep down, not visible for the outside world.

When I was going through dark times and experiencing depressive episodes, realizing and facing what made me feel this particular way was the steppingstone toward healing. I figured I couldn't beat this myself, and denying I was not okay made everything worse.

I believe part of why Chris' career didn't take off in a similar direction as his cohort was because he wasn't fully facing depression itself in his life. In a way, his professional career was doomed to failure from the beginning. How can we excel at our craft while still struggling to be the best version of our inner selves? Too often, we don't realize we are our greatest enemies and put a brake on progress but blame the outside world for it while the problem and solution are happening internally.

Although his comedy career was slowly fading away and his name was associated increasingly less with famous comedians,

Chris participated in the Edinburgh Festival Fringe in 2016, performing his show "Career Suicide." This special would create temporary attention. Judd Apatow, famous writer, director, and producer known for blending comedy and tragedy in his movies, was the executive producer eventually broadcast on HBO one year later.

> "One of the things that I realized in the course of doing the show ["Career Suicide"] is how much my coming to grips with stuff was realizing that I'm not gonna beat this [depression]. I'm not gonna win. I don't get to erase this part of my brain. It's there, so I just have to learn to live with it, face it down and navigate my life with it."
>
> —Chris Gethard

The loyal east coast-based comedian, who has struggled with mental health issues since adolescence, may not be the first to perform standup about depression. Still, he's one of the very few who has boldly made it the core piece of a mainstream comedy special. Chris has accepted that going through depressive episodes will always be a part of his life, and it is nothing to be embarrassed about. He just chooses a different approach dealing with it now by openly addressing it through the use of comedy.

He still finds humor while living with his demons and defiantly smiles as he tries to erase the stigma around mental illness. Not the picturesque ending you might have expected reading this, but that's the ironic link between comedy and tragedy.

FACING THE FEAR AND ANXIETY OF THE UNKNOWN

"It is absolutely, positively a coping mechanism. This is my therapy."

—FRANTZ CAYO

Although I never shared a comedy class with Frantz, I am lucky enough to have met him along the way of writing this book. Frantz started learning standup at one of New York City's most famous venues, the Gotham Comedy Club. It was always part of his bucket list to do a live performance, whether he would like it or not.

When my first standup show came up, I didn't know whether I would love or hate it. All I knew was I *had* to do it. It was some sort of calling that told me to go out on that stage and perform. If I had bombed miserably, at least I would have had a fantastic story to tell at dinner parties. Or the experience could have been so great it would make me want to go back in front of an audience the next day. As history has shown, the latter scenario happened.

Diving into this unique world ignited that same spark for Frantz that unleashed my passion for it when I took my first class in LA. It made him always come back to the stage despite all the difficulties and uncertainties standup comedy entails. "Comedy is difficult, but so is life. So much uncertainty, loss, and fear in both realms," he said to me.

Dealing with ambiguity isn't easy for anybody. But for some, it is precisely what makes us feel alive. Let me assure you: Doing routines alone on stage is the most dubious thing you can do. You may know what you're going to talk and joke about, but you have no idea how the audience will perceive it, let alone like it, and laugh about it. You might forget a line or have to deal with hecklers and master those situations on the spot.

Standup comedy is one of the most straightforward crafts there is. You receive instant, live feedback while you're in the act. This kick makes me and many others who pursue and share the same devotion for it feel invincible.

Frantz has been anxious since he was a young boy. Yet, once he took his first step into that New York City comedy club, collecting waves of laughter has been a tempering valve because it gives him an outlet to write and express openly what he thinks and feels. While his wife wanted him to seek professional help initially, he used his pain as a source for his creativity.

> "My wife keeps on saying either go to a therapist or get medicine or whatever. I'm like, nope, they'll slow me down. I don't want to do that. I'm just gonna pour it into the comedy."
>
> —Frantz Cayo

Standup always has been a way for him to stay away from drug therapy. It was and still is self-therapy, not to mention it is also less expensive. Yet, the exciting thing is that although many comedians do talk about their personal life or their trauma, Frantz uses it as an opportunity to talk about so much more. It is his platform and way to address social issues that concern him. He is trying to deal with that corresponding anxiety by making fun of it. It is his chance to tell jokes about false promises society makes. That same community that let him down too many times, so he can subside the actual anger and despair inside of him. Writing a joke about these issues and sharing it with the world is his way of keeping sane.

Consequently, the best comedy is when people can feel like they're getting to know you. The more personal it is, the more universal it becomes. Frantz is doing precisely this. There is a caveat, though. For many comedians, their creative writing originated out of pain, whether it is mental, physical, or social. Hopefully, that sorrow will be gone at one point, but we need the creativity to stick.

Suppose a comedian's inner pain starts to alleviate and fade away, which obviously is a good thing. Yet, in that case, if they become too successful, their comedic material might suffer. It's a paradox because chances are they're not perceived as funny anymore. It's tragic to think that once someone has worked out their issues and might even become known and popular for their unique style, their wit seems to peel off because they have nothing for the audience to relate to anymore.

Yet, I believe once comics reach this point, they start to diversify. Famous comedians usually go into acting. Then it is not about them writing or performing their pain. They're now portraying it and assume any role another person wants them to be. Because once you're no longer hungry and suffering, what are you going to authentically write about?

CREATIVITY IS A TWO-EDGED SWORD

Like Chris and Frantz, more people try comedy as a way *out* of whatever circumstances they are in or a way *into* what they think is the glamorous and exciting world of entertainment. There is a dangerous side effect to it, though, that comes with the constant pressure of squeezing our right side of the brain to be ever more creative.

For many, the desire to feel okay or just less troubled can manifest itself in performance and creative work. Nevertheless, there is a high chance that it will manifest itself in harmful behavior, like a drug or alcohol addiction. One reason why so many people turn to substance abuse when they fall prey to any kind of personal problem is that it temporarily takes away the pain. Still, whether the argument is true that drug habits have led to extraordinary pieces of art, it is undeniably true that in the end, harmful substances always beat art and its creators.

It is a common belief but also a misconception that these substances liberate creativity. Zsolt Demetrovics, a Hungarian clinical psychologist and director of the Institute of Psychology at the Eötvös Loránd University in Budapest, Hungary, contradicted this belief in his 2016 published study *Creativity and Psychoactive Substance Use: A Systematic Review*.

> The general results suggest that there is an association between creativity and substance use. However, the studies were unable to show that substance use directly contributed to the growth of creativity or facilitated creative artistic process. It is concluded that specific skills may be subject to change as a

consequence of substance use, and consequently may have an effect on the style of creation.

People may debate that Jean-Michel Basquiat needed heroin to paint or John Belushi needed cocaine and alcohol to do comedy. Yet, it is worth remembering that in the end, it killed them both as it took too many other talented creative geniuses. Addiction is a disease, not a shortcut to fame and success.

Johns Hopkins University School of Medicine neuroscientist David Linden states that humans don't have one single specific gene for addiction. It is not something we are born with or that can be passed on. However, some individuals may have a genetic makeup that gives them a lower functioning dopamine system.

Suppose a person's dopamine system isn't correctly working or is just not strong enough to release a sufficient amount. In that case, it guides that person to more risk-taking and compulsive behavior. Simultaneously, a dopamine deficiency is considered one chemical cause for depression. Hence, these risk-tolerant drives can be a potential catalyst for creativity and addiction.

Another cause for artists engaging in substance abuse is the way they process information differently. They see the world around them from a different perspective and are able to think outside the box. This, however, can produce dangerous side effects, which is where the real risks of creativity lie.

Looking at the world from another angle can also dilute our views and opinions on common rules and norms within society. The ability to evade certain rules and create one's own requires a high level of imagination. Phrases such as "rules are meant to be broken" and "ask for forgiveness, not permission" sit at the core front of new creations.

I don't have to make a secret that heavy alcohol and drug abuse is ubiquitous and clearly visible in the LA comedy scene. I'm not a saint myself, but I always manage to keep any harmful substances or behavior on a healthy, or at least not damaging level, as ironically as this may sound. Their struggle with narcotics is so present in many of my fellow comics' lives because apart from dealing privately with their own issues, they also have to deal with the rest of the world knowing about it.

As a comic, you're a lone wolf in a large herd. You're chasing and running toward the same prey but end up alone and miserable in your cave at the end of the day. After performing on stage, the high you get can transform into your darkest fear once you're back in your apartment, hotel room, or whatever you may call home. This is the moment where many comedians are most vulnerable, in my opinion. The spotlight is off, but you just want to feel admired and appreciated again. A feeling that many mistakenly think can be replicated by reaching for that bottle of vodka, a bag of coke, or heroin needle, all of which are also common visitors in the green room.

You see, all I just talked about had *everything* to do with the environment we were living in. My greatest strength in this hilarious world of temptation was that I found friends I could make meaningful connections with who lifted me up while I was down and grounded me when I was too close to potentially hurting myself. Whatever addiction, sickness, or hardship you might go through, know there are others who care. Reaching out is not a sign of weakness but of great strength.

Creativity is a two-edged sword. Without visionary and bold people, our world would be monotonous and doomed to failure. It brings disruption and innovation into our world. However, precisely this impact can become a great danger for gifted and visionary people and their followers as they start to form their own reality.

In this new world, the rules and regulations of the societies we live in don't apply anymore. The perspective on what's good and bad is entirely rethought. Bad behavior such as harming one's own body through any kind of drug use can be easily justified. We should and always will appreciate any form of originality in our world, but stop glorifying and justifying the great tragedies that tend to follow it yet too often.

CORE LESSONS
- Creativity is a two-edged sword.

- Addiction is a disease, not a shortcut to success.

- Alcohol and drug use don't help foster the creative process.

PART 3

COMEDY IS FUNNY...AND SO MUCH MORE

CHAPTER 7

THE C IN COMEDY IS FOR CONNECTION

> "There's a whole series of things you can perform on stage so that the average audience doesn't get too freaked out. They're just not used to having that kind of emotion come up in a conversation or pretty much ever. I mean, some people just either avoid it, or it never comes up in their lives. They just don't think about it, they just don't deal with it."
>
> —Bill Bernat

There is one endeavor in the discussion around mental health that is given too little attention in an effort to fight its attached stigma. I am talking about (better) *connecting* with people struggling with their inner demons. Empathizing with those suffering plays as big of a role as curing the disease itself. Yet, researchers and doctors around the world put most of their focus into *solving* the problem, rather than *helping* people live with it. You might think this is intuitive, and it sure is in the long-term. However, with hundreds of millions of people going through sorrow right now, there needs to be an immediate solution or approach to supporting those in need.

Bill Bernat is one of those people who stands on both sides of the spectrum. He's been fighting and living with his psychiatric illness all his life. He is also a mental health advocate trying to lighten and simplify the discussion around depression and anxiety. Bill began battling his bipolar disorder when he was just eight years old. At the time of our interview, he told me he is now twelve years clean from addiction, which resulted from his mental health condition in the first place. After going through suicide attempts and drug overdoses, Bill built a new life and learned how to stay well with his Bipolar 2 Disorder.

A Bipolar 2 condition differs from a Bipolar 1 condition in how it is defined by a pattern of depressive and hypomanic episodes, but not the full-blown manic experience typical of Bipolar I Disorder (National Institute of Mental Health, 2020). During a hypomanic event, your energy level is increased, and mood is elevated to some degree. However, this behavior can still be viewed as "normal" by the people around you, making it even harder for others to fully grasp the severity of this disease.

Bill has been on an odyssey through depression, addiction, and social anxiety his entire life. Yet, he has made it his purpose to educate and teach others about living well with their maladies. He quickly realized that before we can cure such a disease, we need to fully understand it and, more importantly, empathize with those who go through it.

CONNECTING THROUGH COMEDY: FINDING HUMOR WITHIN AND WITH OTHERS

Along his way of fighting this stigma, educating others, and helping those in need, Bill found a common thread that would always be present. It was finding the humor within. Although he experienced severe social anxiety when he was younger, he still tried to do standup comedy. He knew he wouldn't be able to connect with crowds on a very deep level. Yet, he enjoyed doing it as it allowed him to process his emotions at different levels.

Thinking about the first time I went on stage gives me this tickling feeling in my stomach to this day. As I'm writing about it, I am full of excitement and would do anything for this pandemic to be over so I can perform in front of a live audience again. It was an emotional rollercoaster. Even though the local comedy club only gave me three minutes for my standup debut, it felt like a century on stage. Time works differently up there. What I was gifted with was three minutes of pure, undivided attention from seventy people I had never met in my life. Yes, I had friends and family come to my show too. But trying to give a speech even in front of your loved ones can be a great challenge. And here I was, trying to make them laugh. It was terrifying yet thrilling.

I always like to draw the connection between performing comedy on stage and posting something on social media, let's say Instagram. Both are a form of personal expression. What most people don't realize, though, is how much responsibility comes when engaging on these platforms. The number of followers always plays a role. But no matter how big or small this number is, your voice will be heard. If you think your opinion can't make a difference because only 150 people follow you, I advise you to think again. Imagine giving a speech on stage in front of 150 people. You would think twice about what your next sentence will be.

> "A lot of people do standup because they have a deep-seated unmet need for attention and approval for whatever reason. Everybody's got their own personal story about their childhood and their upbringing and whatever makes their psyche in the present day."
>
> —Bill Bernat

The other benefit standup comedy provided was happening off stage. For Bill and many others, it was spending time and hanging out with other comics. It was an opportunity to bond over whatever was going on in their lives, whatever they were struggling with, which mostly was trauma or other severe setbacks. Within this safe zone, or how I like to call it "the treehouse of trust," they could be these slightly dysfunctional people but comfortable being around each other.

Bill described it as a group of freaks, but they were all kind of weirdos in the same way. Finding a way to connect on such a deep and personal level has been really helpful to him and many other comedians. It perfectly describes the beauty of comedy in relationship with mental health.

As a comic, you continuously try to push society's boundaries with whatever topic is considered taboo at the time. When Bill started doing standup comedy, he would perform his stories about journeys through mental struggles and addiction. He tested the limits. This "darkness" is not dark to him, though. It's the world he has been living in almost his entire life. It is the world that he sees. Through standup, he realized he could communicate to a broader audience about controversial subjects like personality disorders.

By doing comedy myself, I learned the audience of people who deal with depression and anxiety is a lot bigger than people admit and might think. In the comedy world of mental health, there is the spectrum of:

a. humor that only people who have been going through mental hardships will understand and...

b. humor that everybody else gets.

Within these cornerstones, stories told through standup comedy can be relatable to anyone. This is what makes it real, authentic, and captivating.

For most people, connecting and bringing forward these experiences is universal. Even if you haven't been suicidal, you have felt down. Even if you don't have social anxiety, you have felt awkward or like an outsider who doesn't fit in. Ultimately, it is these universal experiences that connect us which make humor so valuable and important. If someone feels alone or disconnected because he or she may experience these conditions, humor can show them that other people go through the same. It's both the humor and the corresponding relief that provides healing powers.

STAY AWESOME: MENTAL HEALTH TRENDS

Mental health is no longer a stranger to standup comedy. In fact, comedians are sharing their experiences during live shows, podcasts, and talk shows now more than ever. Whether it is Chris Gethard's 2019 HBO special *Career Suicide*, John Moe's book *The Hilarious World of Depression*, or Marc Maron's podcast "WTF with Marc Maron," mental health is an integral element of today and tomorrow's comedy shows.

> "I think it's a reflection of a general trend in society to be more open about mental health issues. People realize that it's not that uncommon and that everybody is impacted by it. The current Zeitgeist is that it's okay to mention these things."
>
> —Bill Bernat

The trend that an increasing number of comedians are opening up about mental health is standing on the shoulders of solid research and science. Based off research in 2020, the National Alliance on Mental Illness (NAMI) reports that one in five people will experience some sort of mental illness each year. The implications of COVID-19 and its corresponding mental health risks due to social isolation will only fuel this negative trend further (Panchal et al, 2020). In a nutshell, these conditions are widely common. Nonetheless, "Mental disorders are the most neglected of the global health problems," says Vikram Patel, MBBS, PhD, a psychiatrist and professor of global health and social medicine at Harvard Medical School.

It is still an uphill battle as most people who are not directly affected by it don't want to deal with depressed people at all.

We are still a far cry from the ultimate goal of total acceptance everywhere. I'm afraid that while you currently read this book and may even experience depression, you might still get judged. You probably will still be discriminated against and excluded by some people. The silver lining, though, is that the number of people criticizing others with depression is shrinking each day. At the same time, the number of people who will include and accept you is growing.

Through initiatives such as Stay Awesome by Bill Bernat and many others, voices around mental health become louder, clearer, and reach people that seemed to be unreachable a decade ago. Stay Awesome is a workshop led by Bernat that makes subjects like depression and anxiety easy to talk about among friends and co-workers.

There's no reason in nature or in our DNA for this to be judged in any way. It is one hundred percent a man-made phenomenon. Because he has been in the world for mental health advocacy half of his life, Bill lost touch to the fact that people are supposed to be embarrassed about their conditions. Our society is also improving in realizing there is no need for this disconnect to exist. It is finally starting to shift.

The irony behind it is that the one thing depressed and anxious people need more than anything else to heal is a meaningful connection to others. Yet, society and culture have been dealing with these issues by excluding and stigmatizing people.

In sum, what this movement is driven by and what it comes down to is immediate compassion. Standup comedy sits at the forefront of vulnerability and openness about such topics.

This reflects a more significant societal trend. Comedians' talents will bring us closer to believe that all people who deal with mental health problems should be accepted and included.

REDUCING STIGMA THROUGH SHARING

As much as curing psychological illnesses remains a significant challenge, so does fighting its attached stigma and discrimination. Employers are still underestimating the impact poor mental health has on personnel productivity within the professional world. One of the biggest reasons is that they lack an accurate picture of the problem.

Fortunately, as I mentioned earlier in this chapter, current generations shift toward a more compassionate and more educated society. Generation Z, in particular (anyone born between 1997 and 2015, nearly sixty-eight million people in the US), will lead this shift. In fact, mental health stigma is fading for Gen Z (Bethune, 2020). Compared to previous generations, Gen Z not only has a greater acceptance for mental health issues, but they are also more likely to report mental health problems and actively seek treatment partly because of positive media influences.

"I think you are seeing this shift where celebrities, movie stars, TV stars, and star athletes are being more open and writing articles about mental health," says Dr. Caroline Vaile Wright, director of research and special projects at the American Psychology Association (APA). "They're posting on social media about mental health. I think we see this possible reduction in stigma around mental health and more openness to discussing it than we have in the past."

As the saying goes, "Time is a great healer." We will see an increased acceptance, a fading, and hopefully entirely removed stigma within the next few decades. Generations to come will enter this world with greater awareness. Even nowadays, children are being asked in school to rate their mood every day.

However, the question remains why mental health stigmas exist in the first place. Interestingly enough, people who are too afraid to face their own pain are a big contributor to the overall problem. I believe some of it comes from people who don't want to look at their own pain. They don't want to look at their shadows. These people may be the hardest ones to reach, and it may take longer for them to change. However, in order to have meaningful and sustainable improvement, we have to show them that it is okay to have a battle against ourselves.

At the same time, most of the prejudices and biases still come from older generations and earlier days in which misguided views have been passed along. People thought and still partly believe that these individuals were "different" from everyone else. They would be described as lunatics or even accused of demonic or spiritual possession.

"In my parents' generation, crazy people got stuck in a fucking hospital where they got chained to the wall and electrocuted and lobotomized," says Chris Gethard. It was not only people's perception of others struggling with their mental health, but also an entire health care system held onto these views and beliefs, hence creating this stigma.

As time progresses, we will see more stories surface. Those affected will start to realize their conditions are just as usual as other more commonly accepted health problems. In fact, it is not something new. They've been working and living alongside people like this all the time; it just hasn't come out in conversation often enough. Consequently, stories will play a crucial part.

The comic is a talented and honest storyteller. No matter if you've gone through similar situations to what was described in an experience or not, you become emotionally connected to it. This can ultimately change the way we hear and think about them. They are not a number in another big statistic anymore. They are genuine people with real problems and emotions.

The more people, including comics and others in the limelight, that share their authentic stories, the more compassionate people will become toward mental health challenges. But remember, you don't have to be a comedian, actor, or singer to make a real impact, but just a human being.

CORE LESSONS
- Connection with the ones who suffer plays a crucial part in curing mental health conditions.

- Many people do standup because they have a deep-seated, unmet need for attention and approval for whatever reason.

- Universal experiences connect us, which makes humor valuable and important.

- It's both the humor and the corresponding relief that provide healing powers.

- To be more open about mental health issues reflects a general trend in society.

- Gen Z not only has a greater acceptance for mental health issues, but they are also more likely to report mental health problems and actively seek treatment partly because of positive media influences.

CHAPTER 8

COMEDY IS FUNNY... AND SO MUCH MORE

"The great part about comedy is anyone can do it. It's free. It costs nothing and you need nothing to do it."

—ZEV BURTON

The combination of comedy with any subject or issue is one that people easily overlook. We sometimes tend to seek so desperately to solve a problem, even though the answer is right there within us. Comedy is no longer left for comedians, actors, or other people in the artistic expression, but can be used by everyone in any given moment. Zev Burton is a fellow author I interviewed who wrote a book about the role of humor in international relations. I started this chapter with his quote because it entails the core message: The use of comedy is free, and anyone can do it. We just need to apply it.

SAME BUT DIFFERENT: HUMOR AND COMEDY

There is a difference between comedy and humor that I want to clarify right away. Humor is something rooted in our personality. We are all born with the human ability to experience and express fun. Throughout our childhood and adolescence, we eventually develop a specific sense of humor influenced by the people we grow up with and the circumstances we live in. Even though we might not agree with every kind or see it in every person, it is there within all of us. It relies upon profoundly understanding ourselves and others. It is the ability to read and understand the nature of a given situation and react to it.

Nowadays, people who know me and my stepfather always tell me we have the same sense of humor. It is a unique sarcastic yet witty kind that I started copying and acquiring as I met him when I was a young boy.

On the other hand, comedy is an *expression* of humor. Whereas humor happens more subconsciously and sometimes unintentionally, comedy is the intended act designed to make others laugh. That is why it is a skill that can be learned, trained, and fine-tuned.

Someone who is writing or performing comedic material can become a better writer or performer with time and the necessary education. A writer can become good at comedy through practice, whereas they can't necessarily become good or better at humor. It is considered a form of art rather than an internalized trait. However, it all relies upon and goes back to one's developed sense of humor as comedy builds on exactly this. Your comedic expression can flourish based on your specific taste in humor and how you developed it in the first place.

HEALING THROUGH HUMOR

Humor is a powerful tool on the individual level. It can show great healing qualities, both physically and mentally. A daily dose of comic relief can have real positive impacts on our longevity. Of course, there is nothing funny about a life-changing diagnosis affecting you or a loved one. While humor can't cure our ailments, laughter is proven to improve overall mood, boost our immune systems, and soothe tension caused by stress.

"Heightened stress magnifies the risk of cardiovascular events, including heart attacks and strokes," says Dr. Michael Miller, a cardiologist at the University of Maryland School of Medicine in Baltimore. His research showed that laughter releases nitric oxide, a chemical that relaxes blood vessels, reduces blood pressure, and decreases clotting. Findings from the Yamagata Study, an epidemiological study of Japan's elderly population, published ten years later confirmed that those who tend to laugh more have a lower risk of major cardiovascular illness. It showed that all-cause mortality and cardiovascular disease incidence were significantly higher among subjects with a low frequency of laughter within one month. Therefore, having one good belly laugh a day that sometimes even brings tears to our eyes is a winning strategy to stay healthy in the long run.

On the emotional level, especially during turbulent times like a pandemic or economic crisis, humor is an efficient way to relieve stress and anxiety and release the grip on mental pain. By activating the release of endorphins, it helps us to bring back a sense of normalcy during times with high uncertainty and cope with emotional distress.

Yet just like we can still feel lonely in a room with fifty people we have no meaningful connection with, laughter needs to *come from the heart* to relieve pain. A team of Swiss researchers reported that only "real" delight, actually experienced and accompanied by a Duchenne expression, can increase pain tolerance and improve quality of life (Nikopoulos, 2017).

A "Duchenne smile" not only pulls the corners of our mouth upward but also reaches our eyes, making the corners wrinkle up with crow's feet. It is considered to be among the most influential of human expressions. Hence, a fake smile and laughter, as well as fake friends, don't do any good for our overall health.

Beyond that, humor can also be a great tool on the global stage, bringing peace across international borders to create solidarity. Even though humor differs across countries and cultures, it unites us in its own special ways. It is a useful and effective communication tool and a potential change agent. It expands its value far beyond its expected role as entertainment.

IF WE DON'T LAUGH, WE CRY

> *"Everything can be taken from a man but one thing: the last of human freedoms—to choose one's attitude in any given set of circumstances, to choose one's own way."*
>
> —VIKTOR E. FRANKL

An essential part of a person's attitude is humor. The ability to make fun of yourself at any given moment can be crucial to survival, as Viktor Frankl, Austrian psychiatrist, author, and Holocaust survivor pointed out. In any oppressed situation, coping with it through fun and wit can make it less painful and even uplifting.

Tragically enough, the Jewish people during the Holocaust strengthened their survival instinct through the use of humor. Argentinian author Lazaro Droznes portrayed that will to survive in his 2018 released book *Jewish Humor in the Holocaust: Humor as a Survival Strategy*. The way any dictator or oppressor keeps their power is by depriving people of humanity. Yet, if a person can make themselves or others laugh during these situations, as grotesque as it may seem, any attempt of dehumanization may prove futile.

Furthermore, no dictator can clamp down on humor as it would make them look even more ridiculous. Oppressed people can preserve their dignity through farce and doing comedy. There is nothing else that can make a human feel more as a person than being funny. Fun can transform pessimism into optimism. Submission into resistance. Pain into comfort.

Once you start learning how to be funnier or use humor in your everyday life, you will notice positive changes in your internal and external world. It can feel risky at first telling jokes that violate our psychological safety or even be self-deprecating. Still, it will leave you feeling and being seen as more confident by others because you show the courage to attempt a joke at all. If there are days that you feel like the world is against you or you just feel unhappy with yourself, try to see these things in a humorous light. Turning your fears into something hilarious and using laughter to defeat your dark thoughts will help you project confidence and self-esteem into your life. The reason for this is because the cognitively demanding aspect of applying humor distracts others and yourself, leaving you less able to focus on the negative things happening within and around you.

As comedian Stephen Colbert observes:

> *"You can't laugh and be afraid at the same time—of anything. If you're laughing, I defy you to be afraid."*

Whenever you experience another dark day or something terrible happening to you or a loved one, I encourage you to write something humorous about it as hard as it may seem. It can be as simple as a one-liner in your notes app, or an entire paragraph handwritten on a piece of paper. Find that tiny bit about that bad person or situation that can make the corners of your mouth go up, even if it's just for a few seconds. Positive, good-natured humor in response to tragic news will make you feel better in the absurdity of life.

FAILURE AND RESILIENCE

> *"Standup comedy is an art form, and it dies unless you expand it."*
>
> —SAM KINISON

In the life of a standup comedian, it's not all about the joyful moments. These instants being the center of attention, an audience hysterically laughing at one's jokes, and, in some cases, making a living out of it; this is how usually non-comedians picture a standup comedian's life circumstances.

However, the reality is quite the opposite. If that should even happen, the road to success is a tedious and merciless one, paved with many closed doors and setbacks. It is about failure and perseverance

To any (future) entrepreneur who is reading this right now: Does this sound familiar? After graduating with a master's degree in entrepreneurship and having built businesses myself, this is exactly what my life looked like and still does every time I try to create something new, whether it is a joke or a business idea. Along the way of doing standup comedy, I realized doing comedy makes me a better entrepreneur.

Standup comedy needs to be applied to other areas in life to survive through time. It is an artistic expression and art form too valuable to be reserved for comics only. Talented and famous comedian Sam Kinison pointed this out early in his career in the late 1970s and early 1980s. He was known for his intense and often insulting comedy style, which would colorfully express America's middle-class soul and pain. Being controversial and politically incorrect, yet brutally honest and authentic, Robin Williams even called him the white Richard Pryor.

I found the skills necessary to be a standup comedian useful and practical in the world of entrepreneurship. Certain steps along the way between building a company and performing a comedy routine are very equal. In a way, a comedian's handbook can work for an entrepreneur and vice versa.

NO ONE IS BORN A MASTER

You have to start from scratch. Whether it is coming up with a new joke or a business idea, it all starts with a pen and a piece of paper. Sometimes, such ideas come to you out of the blue, and you sketch it on the back of a napkin at a restaurant. You never know when it's going to hit you, but when it does, it is like enlightenment: a spark that can burst into creative flames.

Preparation is key in almost everything. It starts with finding new material. But how do you find these elements that make a joke a joke? Be as observing and attentive as you possibly can; about yourself, about others, about social and political conditions. If there is something that upsets you in your relationship, write it down and bring it up. You can't stand how some people are being treated in your community? Write it down and bring it up. You want to openly address your government's flaws? Write it down and bring it up (unless you live in a communist country like North Korea, in which case you might want to think twice about what you can and cannot say for the sake of your personal well-being).

By writing something down, you set the steppingstone in what could become a hilarious joke or brilliant business idea. What I'm saying here is there is a message in every standup comedy routine. It is something you genuinely care about and, in some cases, want to change for the better.

Similarly, entrepreneurs encounter a problem and make it their personal mission to solve this for the greater good. It is the passion for a specific solution that turns an idea into a running company. It is that same passion for certain circumstances, conditions, or experiences that a standup comedian inhabits and will lead to great jokes.

As entrepreneurs or comedians, we have lived through whatever we talk and preach, so there is authenticity in our content, which people can relate to. Addressing things people are shying away from saying or haven't noticed yet themselves is a talent any great comedian and entrepreneur has. It requires a tremendous amount of soul searching and observation skills.

There are times when I spent three hours writing one line, which I thought was hilarious, just to realize later that the line isn't working in a live show. It was pretty much the same feeling when I pitched one of my well thought-through business ideas to investors, and all they would leave me with is "Oh, I've seen that already. How will you be different from your competitors?" All the investors see is a nicely made pitch deck and me giving a presentation. What they don't see are the many sleepless nights, headaches, rehearsals, and feedback that went into it.

The same goes for comedians. Although it might look extremely natural and with ease, comedians prepare for months or even years in advance, fine-tuning their sets based on different audience's reactions. During a performance by Dave Chappelle at The Comedy Store in LA, which was also the first time I saw Chappelle live, he said that on average, it takes a whole year to write a "perfect" sixty-minute Netflix special. Out of personal experience, I could very much relate to it as it took me almost six weeks to come up with five minutes of material for one of my first shows.

The good news is, you don't need to be a comedian to be funny and find absurdity in sorrow. All that matters is whatever you think is funny; it's funny to *you*. Even a hilarious memory will do and bring some levity into the yet-so-serious world we sometimes think we live in. It may be a shocker for you now, but none of us will make it out of this world alive, so let's use comedy as a vehicle to make it less painful.

PERSEVERANCE IS KEY

Being both a great comedian and entrepreneur requires you to have thick skin. These professions are nothing for highly sensitive people. Loud boos or a failed deal should fuel your fire to continue and keep doing what you love. If you look at it differently, rejection is nothing else than valuable real-life feedback from the market or your audience, allowing you to fine-tune and improve your product or routine.

As a standup comedian, you start performing your rough draft in front of other comedians during an open mic or even in front of a small audience. Many people don't understand that a comedian's set within a certain period of time is more or less the same. Occasionally there will be another joke added or a line cut. The core, though, is practicing the same routine to perfect it. A rough first draft is becoming a comedic masterpiece through these tiny precise changes based on fellow comedians' and audiences' reactions and feedback.

What a first draft is for a comedian is a prototype for the entrepreneur. This means that it is just good (or funny) enough to do the job. Is it perfect? Absolutely not. But it is something to work with. No entrepreneur will just toss their prototype and develop a whole new idea because of lousy feedback or naysayers. It allows them to cater to what the customer really needs.

On the other hand, once an entrepreneur or comedian has reached a certain level of success, the job is not done. As hard as you might have worked for your success, it's just as difficult, sometimes more so, to maintain it. Particularly famous comedians who are regularly exposed to the public know that one single misstep can boomerang them back to square one. However, and that is the beauty of show business, a single performance can also mean the breakthrough of someone's career. Simultaneously, one brilliant idea sketched in a college dorm room can turn into a billion-dollar business.

SERIOUSLY FUNNY

Although we sometimes find ourselves laughing alone when we think of a funny situation or watch a hilarious movie, real laughter primarily happens during social interactions with others. Yet, at least during pre-pandemic times, our workplace is amid a humor drought for most people. A recent study of Gallup data for the US found that we laugh significantly less on weekdays than we do on weekends.

It is tragic to think the one place we spend the most time during our week, and for many people during their entire life, is a place in which fun is considered inappropriate.

Fortunately, some people devote their life to find and apply humor in these situations and circumstances. The goal is obviously not to undermine the seriousness of an important business meeting but to create a happier, healthier, and thus more efficient environment for both employers and employees.

Jamie Anderson is one of those people who considers himself like a comedy consultant. In his 2018 eponymous TEDx Talk "The Standup Strategist: Leading with Humour," Jamie shares the findings of his research on the core benefits of humor in the workplace, as well as an intuitive framework for its application in leadership. Originally from Australia and now living and working in Antwerp, Netherlands, as a professor of strategic management at Antwerp Management School, he found four core areas in both our professional and personal lives that can be considerably boosted through the use of humor:

- Community
- Coping
- Change
- Creativity

Particularly as a leader or person in charge, appropriately "joking around" with employees, interns, or people considered to be "below" that person shows humility, openness, and the desire to bond. In standup, a joke is built in three parts: premise, setup, punchline. The premise and setup build tension, and the punchline eventually releases it. When you or your boss start releasing this initial tension prevalent in many business meetings through a joke, it'll make thought processes flow better and create a more trusting environment.

Business can be stressful. We've all been in situations where our heart rates increased, our hands started getting sweaty, and we were feeling a little hot suddenly. Humor is useful to escape this physical and mental state. Studies show that individuals with high levels of humor cope better with demanding and challenging circumstances such as giving presentations or meeting deadlines than individuals with low humor levels. However, be cautious with sarcastic humor or cynicism, which can lead to precisely the opposite of what you might have tried to achieve.

> *"When you want change to happen, it's all about communication because you want people to remember the message."*
>
> —JAMIE ANDERSON

Communication is critical for so many things in our lives. However, being a good communicator requires years of training and experience. The most prominent reason people resist change, particularly within an organization, is that the message hasn't been communicated clearly, leading to fear and aversion toward change.

However, if you can bring humor into your communication style, it helps people understand and process it better. When we think something is funny and laugh, the release of dopamine relaxes not only our physical but also our cognitive tension, which then allows us to be more open toward something new. Once our body is in a relaxed state, and muscles are not tensed anymore, we usually tend to perform better in any kind of physical activity, preventing us from getting injuries.

The same goes for our brain once the cognitive tension is released. The frontal cortex, which is the hub of creativity in our brain and is responsible for many functions that contribute to creative thinking, opens up when being "relaxed." Consequently, making yourself and others laugh leads to overall increased creativity in the room, which can be beneficial for ideation and brainstorming.

The belief that humor is only left for private conversations outside of any professional or "serious" matters is long overhauled. Stanford Graduate School of Business even offers a class on the topic of humor in business called "Humor: Serious Business."

If not misused in a malicious way, humor can make and scale positive change in the world and build more effective and innovative organizations. It provides a different intellectual perspective and makes us carry around a healthy dose of humanity and humility through life.

CORE LESSONS
- Humor is something rooted in our personality. It is the ability to read and understand the nature of a given situation and react to it.

- Comedy is an expression of humor. Whereas humor happens more subconsciously and sometimes unintentionally, comedy is the intended act designed to make others laugh.

- A daily dose of comic relief can have real positive impacts on our longevity.

- While humor can't cure our ailments, laughter is proven to improve overall mood, boost our immune systems, and soothe tension caused by stress.

- Those who tend to laugh more have a lower risk of major cardiovascular illness.

- Humor is an efficient way to relieve stress and anxiety and release the grip on mental pain.

- Finding the humor in tense situations and, to some extent, performing comedy can be very effective in international conflicts to disarm one's enemy. It diffuses the tension around controversial and dangerous topics and can make the difference between war and peace.

- Attitude is the last thing humans have real control over no matter what they have lost or what has been taken away from them.

- There is nothing else that can make a human feel more human than being funny. Humor can transform pessimism into optimism. Submission into resistance. Pain into comfort.

- Along the way of doing standup comedy, I realized doing comedy makes me a better entrepreneur: It is about failure, perseverance, and resilience.

CHAPTER 9

HUMOR IS HOW WE ALL SURVIVE

> "Either in small or big ways, comedy has kept someone out of depression or suicide or helped them cope with a loss and you remember that. If you can talk about something openly and you find the right way to do it, it takes away all of its power."
>
> —Patton Oswalt

We have heard, and maybe even said it ourselves, all too often: "Just get over it. Don't be dramatic. Think positive." And although listening to Taylor Swift's song "Shake It Off" immediately makes me want to dance and puts me in a great mood, it won't necessarily help someone dealing with depression or anxiety. Now, Tay Tay obviously didn't write this song specifically for people battling psychological conditions. Yet, phrases like these are still too omnipresent within the space of mental health in our society. They tend to do more harm than good to those affected.

Nobody on this Earth is immune to diseases. Yes, some vaccines protect us against illnesses such as hepatitis, the flu, or even COVID-19 to some extent. Still, we are defenselessly exposed to most (deadly) ailments, meaning you, me, and everybody around us could fall sick.

On the one hand, we would never blame a loved one for having cancer. Of course not. What kind of person would possibly do that? Even if we have friends or family members who fell victim to lung cancer because they've been chain smokers all their lives, we will express real and genuine sympathy and our best wishes after hearing about such a diagnosis because it's the right thing to do.

On the other hand, depression can become a fatal disease, just like cancer. In a way, it is even more malicious because it kills in absolute silence. At the same time, I don't want to compare apples with pears here. A disease's viciousness can't be measured on a scale. Yet, the overall perception and attitude toward this condition and people dealing with it need to change fundamentally.

Remember, just because you're not dealing with it now doesn't mean you'll never get it. So why would you treat someone who's struggling through it *differently* or not take it seriously? Nobody chose to be depressed or have any kind of mental illness. Let me assure you, when it comes to feeling happy or being sad, a hundred out of a hundred people choose to be happy.

Yet, people act like it was someone's decision to battle depression and that they are to blame for it. Although we see it becoming better, the stigma attached to mental health problems is still alive and well.

A study done by the American Addiction Centers showed that out of the 2,053 survey respondents, 56 percent say they'd be uncomfortable talking to friends and family about it. Eighty-four percent say they'd be uncomfortable talking to their employer. Another survey revealed that 15 percent of respondents label people with a mental disorder as a burden to society. These results are a clear indication we still have a long way to go.

MENTAL ARMOR

So why am I telling you all this and why did I write an entire book about it? Because if you think about it, humor saves lives. It is how we all survive. I found performing standup comedy and watching other comics on stage soothing for the mind and body. We can find healing in ourselves as individuals as well as in entire societies.

Following the psyche of the comic helped me be more attentive and empathetic toward others who are suffering from this disease and to better understand *my* feelings and emotions, too. Standup comics master the balancing act between comedy and tragedy in a way that helps us know that we are not alone out there with what we're going through. This is not a battle to be fighting alone, but together.

They have this unique talent to point out flaws in society and remind us that if something or somebody just doesn't look right. It is a craft that has evolved into personal storytelling, which helps both the one who is sharing and the listener. Comics are society's individual confessors. They take the hit for all of us and make it easier to understand and cope with whatever is ahead. As history has shown, they have always been agents of change and challenged stereotypes and stigma.

> *"Being a comedian who lives on making fun of everything around him, the ridiculousness of everything, to come through something horrendous and to be alive, you got to have a sense of humor. If you don't, you go mad."*
>
> —RICHARD PRYOR

In the preceding chapters, I have tried to make the general argument for being funnier. Of course, there is nothing funny about mental health problems. Still, the fact that humor's healing powers stand on solid scientific ground is proof it can help you, me, and everyone around us going through emotionally draining times.

There is a pandemic going on right now that has already taken hundreds of thousands of lives, destroyed millions of jobs, and has overthrown every plan we initially made for ourselves. In 2008, we experienced one of history's worst financial crises. Many parts of this world experience civil wars and natural disasters.

Besides hope and the firm belief that we will eventually get out of any tragedy, we need a vehicle that will get us to that point in the first place. Humor is the vehicle that can get us through the darkest hours.

LAUGHTER IS THE BEST MEDICINE

While comedy can't prevent bad things from happening (most of the time), it can support us to relieve stress and anxiety and help lower mental and physical pain. In addition, research from doctors and health experts around the globe show that genuine laughter reduces the risk of major cardiovascular illnesses (heart attack), says Dr. Michael Miller, a cardiologist at the University of Maryland School of Medicine in Baltimore.

On a grander scale, comedy has revealed it can shift entire societies and overthrow regimes. People being heavily oppressed are using humor to transform submission into resistance and turn pessimism into optimism. When we make fun of our fears and see them through the lens of the ridiculous, it can't hurt us anymore. The negative and gloomy outlook we were initially stuck in is entirely shifted once humor comes into play.

Whatever stage in life you are at or circumstances you are coming from, comedy has something for all of us. It doesn't have international borders, skin colors, sexual orientation, or religious beliefs. Quite the contrary, it is something that can connect different cultures and bring together the worst of enemies.

Yet, to have natural healing happening, we need to understand the causes of the problems, too. Depression can come from a chemical dysfunction in our brains; that is correct. We must not overlook that a lot of what causes depression is anchored in our society and environment. Therefore, to tackle something that has social causes, we need to look into social solutions.

Loneliness, for example, is a killer. Although many aspects of our lives have evolved and progressed, specific mechanisms rooted in our DNA from thousands of years ago are still within us *today*. Being separated from their tribes, humans were destined to die. Today, isolation and separation are still leading causes of depression and anxiety, leading to death in the worst cases. Therefore, meaningful connections can both relieve and prevent mental pain from happening.

STANDING UP FOR MENTAL HEALTH

The comic can help us understand the power of unmasking ourselves. Although it can be the scariest thing standing on stage alone in front of tens, hundreds, or thousands of people, this boldness can be a therapeutic experience. Out of personal experience, I can tell you that once you've been up there, you either love it or hate it. There is no maybe. And I loved it! The second I went off stage after my first gig, I knew I'd be back. It is this constant high that comics chase that blocks out everything that's happening around or to us at the time.

Comics are unafraid of any kind of judgment and put themselves in the most vulnerable position possible. Sometimes, they tell their audience their deepest secrets. But, many times, it is something they haven't even told their best friends. On stage, we [comics] liberate our individuality and become ourselves wholly.

By doing comedy, we're not chased by depression and anxiety anymore. By seeing yourself from all perspectives, your inner demons are exposed. They can't hide within us anymore.

What used to control us and our everyday life is now entirely tamed. How much more uncertain can it become than standing in front of hundreds of strangers trying to make every single one of them laugh? Facing the fear of the unknown becomes a comic's best friend.

As I was writing this book, doing my research, and talking to many different people, I realized that we were moving in the right direction. Increasingly more comedians speak up about mental health. Why? Because society's general trend is to be more open about this topic. Standup comedians are the voice of the community—in good and bad times. Do you want to know how we're doing as a society, what our emotional state is? Go watch standup comedy.

This year, the year that I'm writing this book has been a special one for me. I have never been faced with more uncertainty than now. I believe it is an environment that is all too new for billions of people on this planet. Without a doubt, most of what I had initially planned changed. I was forced to rethink and adapt. We like to pretend that we do and feel better when things are predictable and known. However, humans are capable of not only enduring but embracing uncertainty by the most creative means.

Living in Los Angeles and not being able to travel back to Germany because of international travel restrictions separated me from my family like never before. It was, and still is, an emotional roller coaster that some ride better than others. However, the process of writing this book and doing the work helped me not only cope with the new circumstances I'm in but exploit them to my advantage.

Like so many of us under quarantine, I was forced to deal with myself like never before. Although I don't want to say that I became a whole new person, I feel like a different version of the man I was before this entire thing started. I have grown personally and finally found something I wasn't even aware I was searching for in the first place: passion and purpose—a passion for standup comedy and writing that translates into my purpose of bringing out the best in people and making them laugh.

Comedy is so much more than being funny or watching people telling jokes. It is a beautiful way to connect, bring people together, and turn around their burdens with playful relief.

Whatever stage you are in or however you are feeling right now, know you are *never* alone. If you're in a good place right now emotionally, I'm genuinely happy for you. But don't take it for granted. Next time someone's telling you that they are feeling miserable, tell them you care. Listen to understand first and to respond second. There's nothing unusual about feeling lonely and sad at times. Everybody copes differently with sadness and grief. I hope, though, that I was able to show you how uplifting it can be to laugh through tragedy rather than suffer through it.

> *"Everyone you meet is fighting a battle you know nothing about. Be kind. Always."*
>
> —ROBIN WILLIAMS

ACKNOWLEDGMENTS

Writing a book is harder than I thought and more rewarding than I could have ever imagined. None of this would have been possible without the people mentioned next.

I want to start by saying thank you to those reading this who made it to the acknowledgments section. *The Goldfinch* by Donna Tartt was the thirty-seventh best-selling book of 2014 and won the Pulitzer Prize but was only finished by 44 percent of those who started it. *Twelve Years a Slave* by Solomon Northrup was only completed by 28 percent of its readers in that same year. The fact that you actually finished this book and didn't put it away halfway through means the world to me.

Thank you, Mom and Christian, for your unwavering support and unconditional love that helped shape the person I am today and for instilling in me the attitude that I can do whatever I set my mind to. I wouldn't be anywhere close to where I am today without your backing and belief in me.

I want to thank my publisher, New Degree Press, for giving me this opportunity and chance to accomplish something most people will only dream about. Thank you, Eric Koester, for encouraging me to give this book idea a shot and put my story and ideas out into the world. Without the experiences and support from you and the entire NDP team, this book would not exist.

Thank you to my developmental editor Regina Stribling and acquiring editor Lisa Patterson for your editorial help and keen insight in bringing my stories to life. Special thanks to my marketing and revisions editor Alan Zatkow for teaching me what excellent writing is about, keeping me on track through all my revisions, and never giving up on me and *The Ironic Link*.

Thank you, Charles, my neighbor, friend, and ultimate creative mentor, for your generous spirit and teaching me how to unleash my artistic potential and constantly exposing me to new thoughts and ideas.

Thank you, Alex, my classmate, friend, and life coach, for your time and thoughtfulness during every single session. Your sage counsel and guidance made me become a better version of myself.

Thank you, Maryam, my dear friend, for taking a chance on me when I was at my lowest and didn't know any further. Your positivity and constant support are what got me through many struggles during the process of writing this book.

Thank you to the people I interviewed for this book: Dr. Deborah Serani, Dr. Michael P. Mah, Benjamin Houltberg, Ph.D, Bill Bernat, Frantz Cayo, Morgan Michaels, Zev Burton.

Thank you to every single person who shared their excitement with me for *The Ironic Link*, regardless of context, for being a part of my life and teaching me something valuable. I would like to thank everyone who texted, commented, and supported me on this journey. For those who shared *The Ironic Link* with others to help build momentum.

And a special thanks to the following people for participating in my pre-order campaign by buying one or several copies early to make publishing possible. I am sincerely grateful for your generosity:

Felix Beisemann, Luca Mische, Nik Smidt, Douglas Fullerton, Sam Jaschke, Jan Martens, Lara Martens, Kevin Bernatek, Mark Lukas Kadansky, Svenja Krüssenberg, Peter Dozsa, Niclas Baetcher, Niklas Breuker, Carlo Reitano, Jason Buen, Bea Santos, Daniela Pacheco, Serdar Turan, Cilga Turan, Maurice Maschmeyer, Stefan Krause, Claudia Dermutz, Peter Dermutz, Niclas Dermutz, Anna Essers, Josefina Eickhoff, Kai Feld, Joseph Moses, Philipp Krebs, Jigar Patel, Vanessa Meulendik-Bazzo, Nicole Maranca, Katharina Heuermann, Evelyn Hammerstroem, Caroline von Plehwe, Sara Nassehi Nejad, Duygu Altinbasak, Nicki Lange, Shahira Badram, Jorge Fajardo, Victor Niestroj, Rosa Barzegari, Carolin Terhaar, Daisy Bugarin, Mohit Gupta, Gabe Bensimon, Lillian Tsui, Anja Murjahn, Simon Cohen, Jermaine Jackson, Anna Gross, Nertila Asani, Brianna Idelman, Camillo Rohe, Andrea Valdettaro, Daniela Aguin, Sarah Werth, Vivi Uischner, Jeremy Dann, Bernard Komor, Jan Hansen, Robin Averbeck, Andreas Riegler, Tino Calamia, Chien Ya Hsu, Val Semin, Pascal Tait, Paul Willée, Amanda Salvest, Ronny Pannhorst, Victoria Schulz, Alexandra Kano, Shannon Heitmeyer, Fanny

Tousch, Bernadette Niemeyer, Fitore Miftari, Jonathan Keller, Nick Barnett, Sean Todman, Sebastian Krüper, Yan Peter Schreier, Komal Shah, Nick Wagenmann, Kiki Somers, Anika Person, Clara Bühring, Trey Arnold, Zev Burton, Samuel Bartolome, Deirdre Soraci, Chiara Steffling, Melisa Kocakir, Richard Yohannan, Tim Fischer, Natascha Grundmann, Neo Martinez, Judith Dommermuth, Rafael Ortiz Jr, Balint Homonnai Varga, Britta Klotzbach, Ilana Neustadt, Bea Santos, Julie Oberman, Pei Chiang, Eric Koester, Patricia Marie Cruz, Tatiana Safady, Nick Klinger, Issy Berkey, Lauritz Gieseke, Jack Silberman, Cody Shearer, Tiffany Nguyen, Tommy Knapp, Victoria Baehr, Qian Lin, Josefine Kupila, Charles Davis, Verena Sofie Brennecke, Gayaneh Davoodian, Sarah Mock, Ingrid Girod, Sandrine Sarrola, Bruno Sarrola, Julian Sarrola, Steven Mezzacappa, Corinne Auge, Alexander Mokry, Laura Menz, Emanuele Rizzo, Philipp Mühling, Heiner Tent, Kian Zomorrodi, Iris Roschitz-Dey, Christian Roschitz, Jinous Khadivian, Marco Salari, Sheila Pham, Sebastian Doyle, Jeanette Heidewald, Erdavria Simpson, Gracie Lane, Fabian Frehe, Heiko Zhang, Sai Menon, Stas Arsonov, Sabás Leal Ruiz, Kimberly Verge, Nico Taormina, Alex Abramian, Jorg Wallrabe, Maryam Garg, Jose Martin, Katie Hasman, Randolph Zuniga.

APPENDIX

INTRODUCTION

Centers for Disease Control and Prevention. "Mental Health Awareness". Last modified January 20, 2011. Accessed July 19, 2020. https://www.cdc.gov/genomics/resources/diseases/mental.htm.

Gethard, Chris. *Chris Gethard: Career Suicide*. Directed by Kimberly Senior. New York City, NY: Tribeca Performing Arts Center, 2017. https://www.hbo.com/specials/chris-gethard-career-suicide.

Kluth, Andreas. "An Epidemic of Depression and Anxiety among Young Adults." *The Washington Post*, August 24, 2020. https://www.washingtonpost.com/business/an-epidemic-of-depression-and-anxiety-among-young-adults/2020/08/22/dcc06c34-e43c-11ea-82d8-5e55d47e90ca_story.html.

World Health Organization. "Depression." *World Health Organization*, Last accessed September 29, 2021. https://www.who.int/health-topics/depression#tab=tab_1.

World Health Organization. "Mental Health and Psychosocial Considerations during the COVID-19 Outbreak." *World Health Organization,* March 18, 2020. https://apps.who.int/iris/handle/10665/331490.

CHAPTER 1: THE SCIENCE OF DEPRESSION

Fisher, Lauren B., James C. Overholser, Josephine Ridley, Abby Braden, and Cari Rosoff. "From the outside Looking In: Sense of Belonging, Depression, and Suicide Risk." *Psychiatry: Interpersonal and Biological Processes* 78, no 1 (May 2015): 29–41. https://doi.org/10.1080/00332747.2015.1015867.

GoodTherapy, LLC. "Is There a Shortage of Mental Health Professionals in America?" Good Therapy. Last modified March 26, 2020. https://www.goodtherapy.org/for-professionals/personal-development/become-a-therapist/is-there-shortage-of-mental-health-professionals-in-america#:~:text=The%20Substance%20Abuse%20and%20Mental,(60%2C610%20needed%3B%2045%2C210%20available).

Hari, Johann. "This Could Be Why You're Depressed or Anxious." TED. Streamed live on October 11, 2019. YouTube video, 13:50. https://www.youtube.com/watch?v=MB5IX-np5fE&t=405s.

Hellebuyck, Michele, Madeline Halpern, Theresa Nguyen, and Danielle Fritze. *The State of Mental Health in America*. Alexandria, VA: Mental Health America, Inc., 2019. 20. Accessed January 9, 2021. https://www.mhanational.org/sites/default/files/2019-09/2019%20MH%20in%20America%20Final.pdf.

Jamison, Kay R. *Touched with Fire: Manic-Depressive Illness and the Artistic Temperament*. New York: Free Press, 1993.

Jebb, Andrew T., Louis Tay, Ed Diener, and Shigehiro Oishi. "Happiness, Income Satiation and Turning Points around the World." *Nature Human Behaviour*, no 2 (January 2018): 33–38. https://doi.org/10.1038/s41562-017-0277-0.

JRE Clips. "Joe Rogan – Depression Isn't a Chemical Imbalance?" February 12, 2018. Video, 13:19. https://www.youtube.com/watch?v=JniPxNkr_Lk.

Major Depression: The Impact on Overall Health. Chicago, IL: Blue Cross Blue Shield Association, 2018. 3. Published May 10, 2018. https://www.bcbs.com/the-health-of-america/reports/major-depression-the-impact-overall-health.

Maron, Marc. "WTF Episode 106 with Robin Williams." April 26, 2010. In *WTF with Marc Maron*. Produced by Marc Maron. Podcast, MP3 audio, 29:00. https://beta.prx.org/stories/63067.

SoulPancake. "Comedians Tackling Depression & Anxiety Makes Us Feel Seen | Laughing Matters | Documentary." October 10, 2019. Video, 28:49. https://www.youtube.com/watch?v=TBV-7_qGlr4&t=161s.

Ziglar, Zig. *Ziglar on Selling: The Ultimate Handbook for the Complete Sales Professional of the Nineties*. New York: Ballantine Books, 1993.

CHAPTER 2: UNMASKING YOUR TRUE SELF
Bukowski, Charles. *Screams from the Balcony: Selected Letters 1960–1970*. Los Angeles: Black Sparrow Press, 2002.

Bukowski, Charles. *Sifting through the Madness for the Word, the Line, the Way: New Poems*. New York: Ecco Press, 2004.

Maniscalco, Sebastian. *Why Would You Do That?* Directed by Joe DeMaio. New York City, NY: Beacon Theatre, 2016. https://www.netflix.com/mx-en/title/81001278.

Nolan, Christopher, dir. *The Dark Knight Rises*. 2012; Burbank, CA: Warner Bros. Pictures, 2012. Blu-ray Disc, 1080p HD.

CHAPTER 3: DEPRESSION'S UGLY FACE
American Psychology Association. "Childhood Psychological Abuse as Harmful as Sexual or Physical Abuse." American Psychology Association press release, 2014. American Psychology Association website. https://www.apa.org/news/press/releases/2014/10/psychological-abuse#, accessed January 18, 2021.

Beaton, Susan, Peter Forster, and Myfanwy Maple. *Why We Shouldn't Use the 'C' Word*. InPsych, February, 2013.
https://www.researchgate.net/publication/237011391_Suicide_and_Language_Why_we_shouldn't_use_the_'C'_word.

Indian Penal Code Act No. 45 of 1860, Section 309, New Delhi, India: House of Parliament, 1860,
https://indiankanoon.org/doc/1569253/.

SoulPancake. "Comedians Tackling Depression & Anxiety Makes Us Feel Seen | Laughing Matters | Documentary." October 10, 2019. Video, 28:49.
https://www.youtube.com/watch?v=TBV-7_qGlr4&t=161s.

Summit. "Ray Dalio Explains How Pain + Reflection = Progress." January 6, 2019. Video, 1:09.
https://www.youtube.com/watch?v=i4wXCv4GLU0

TEDx Talks. "How to Connect with Depressed Friends | Bill Bernat | TedxSnoisleLibraries." November 21, 2017. Video, 14:05.
https://www.youtube.com/watch?v=m-8tQ_TYLgk&t=149s

UK Legislation, Suicide Act 1961, London, UK: Parliament of the United Kingdom, 1961.
https://www.legislation.gov.uk/ukpga/Eliz2/9-10/60.

CHAPTER 4: THE HISTORY OF COMEDY

Garrison, Greg, dir. *The Dean Martin Show*. Aired September 16, 1965, on NBC.

O'Neill, Tom, dir. *The History of Comedy*. Season 1, episode 1, "F***ing Funny." Aired February 9, 2017, on CNN.
https://www.cnn.com/shows/history-of-comedy.

Sherman-Palladino, Amy, dir. *The Marvelous Mrs. Maisel*. Season 2, episode 2, "Mid-way to Mid-town." Aired December 5, 2018, on Amazon Prime Video.
https://www.primevideo.com/detail/0NHHDAZAX2EG3SK7D9A61KIB1S/ref=atv_nb_lcl_en_US?ie=UTF8.

CHAPTER 5: FEELING HOMESICK AT HOME

Amanda de Cadenet. "Sarah Silverman Gets Real about Depression." November 16, 2015. Video,
https://www.youtube.com/watch?v=M3WZQmRhX10.

Bring Change to Mind. "Wayne Brady: Why I Waited to Talk about My Depression." January 21, 2015. Video,
https://www.youtube.com/watch?v=KFnwJg_4uwM.

Bueno, Antoinette. "Wayne Brady Opens up about His Depression: 'I Had a Complete Breakdown'." *Entertainment Tonight*, November 4, 2014.
https://www.etonline.com/news/153335_wayne_brady_opens_up_about_his_depression.

Gillette, Hope. "Top Relapse Triggers for Depression & How to Prevent Them." *PsychCentral*, April 18, 2021.
https://psychcentral.com/depression/top-relapse-triggers-for-depression-how-to-prevent-them.

Slater, Georgia. "Sarah Silverman Talks Needing to 'Be Funny to Survive' in New Documentary about Mental Health." *People*, October 11, 2019.
https://people.com/health/sarah-silverman-mental-health-documentary-laughing-matters/.

Smith, Dr. Stacy L., Marc Choueiti, Angel Choi, Dr. Katherine Pieper, Dr. Christine Moutier. "Mental Health Conditions in Film & TV: Portrayals That Dehumanize and Trivialize Characters." *USC Annenberg Inclusion Initiative*, (May 2019). https://assets.uscannenberg.org/docs/aii-study-mental-health-media_052019.pdf.

SoulPancake. "Comedians Tackling Depression & Anxiety Makes Us Feel Seen | Laughing Matters | Documentary." October 10, 2019. Video, 28:49. https://www.youtube.com/watch?v=TBV-7_qGlr4&t=161s.

Tull, Matthew T., Kim L. Gratz. "Major Depression and Risky Sexual Behavior among Substance Dependent Patients: The Moderating Roles of Distress Tolerance and Gender." *Cognitive Therapy and Research* 37, (June 2013): 483–497. https://dx.doi.org/10.1007%2Fs10608-012-9490-3.

CHAPTER 6: GO HEAL YOURSELF

Biello, David. "Is There a Link between Creativity and Addiction?" *Scientific American*, July 26, 2011. https://www.scientificamerican.com/article/is-there-a-link-between-creativity-and-addiction/.

Iszáj, Fruzsina, Mark D. Griffiths, and Zsolt Demetrovics "Creativity and Psychoactive Substance Use: A Systematic Review." *International Journal of Mental Health and Addiction*, no. 15 (October 2017): 1135–49. https://link.springer.com/article/10.1007/s11469-016-9709-8#citeas.

O'Neill, Tom, dir. *The History of Comedy*. Season 1, episode 1, "F***ing Funny." Aired February 9, 2017, on CNN. https://www.cnn.com/shows/history-of-comedy.

CHAPTER 7: THE C IN COMEDY IS FOR CONNECTION

Bethune, Sophia. "Gen Z More Likely to Report Mental Health Concerns." *American Psychological Association* 50, no. 1 (January 2020): 20. https://www.apa.org/monitor/2019/01/gen-z.

National Alliance on Mental Illness. "Mental Health by the Numbers." Last updated December 2020. https://www.nami.org/mhstats.

National Institute of Mental Health. "Bipolar Disorder." Last revised January 2020. https://www.nimh.nih.gov/health/topics/bipolar-disorder/index.shtml.

Panchal, Nirmita, Rabah Kamal, Kendal Orgera, Cynthia Cox, Rachel Garfield, Liz Hamel, Cailey Muñana, and Priya Chidambaram. "The Implications of COVID-19 for Mental Health and Substance Use," *Kaiser Family Foundation*, August 21, 2020. https://www.kff.org/coronavirus-covid-19/issue-brief/the-implications-of-covid-19-for-mental-health-and-substance-use/.

SoulPancake. "Comedians Tackling Depression & Anxiety Makes Us Feel Seen | Laughing Matters | Documentary." October 10, 2019. Video, 28:49. https://www.youtube.com/watch?v=TBV-7_qGlr4&t=161s.

Weir, Kirsten. "Elevating Mental Health on the World Stage." *American Psychological Association* 51, no. 1 (January 2020): 44–47. https://www.apa.org/monitor/2020/2020-01-monitor.pdf.

CHAPTER 8: COMEDY IS FUNNY...AND SO MUCH MORE

Beard, Alison. "Leading with Humor." *Harvard Business Review*, May 2014. https://hbr.org/2014/05/leading-with-humor.

Droznes, Lázaro. *Jewish Humor in the Holocaust: Humor as a Survival Strategy.* Scotts Valley: CreateSpace, 2018.

Frankl, Viktor. *Man's Search for Meaning*. Boston: Beacon Press, 2006.

Mehta, Harish C. "Fighting, Negotiating, Laughing: The Use of Humor in the Vietnam War." *The Historian* 74, no. 4 (2012): 743–88. http://www.jstor.org/stable/24455415.

Miller, Michael, William F. Fry. "The Effect of Mirthful Laughter on the Human Cardiovascular System." *Medical Hypotheses* 73, no 5 (November 2009): 636-39. https://doi.org/10.1016/j.mehy.2009.02.044.

Nikopoulos, James. "The Stability of Laughter." *Humor* 30, no 1 (February 2017): 1–21. https://www.degruyter.com/view/journals/humr/30/1/humr.30.issue-1.xml.

Sakurada, Kaori, Tsuneo Konta, Masafumi Watanabe, Kenichi Ishizawa, Yoshiyuki Ueno, Hidetoshi Yamashita and Takamasa Kayama. "Associations of Frequency of Laughter with Risk of All-Cause Mortality and Cardiovascular Disease Incidence in a General Population: Findings from the Yamagata Study." *Journal of Epidemiology* 30, no 4 (April 2020): 188–93. https://doi.org/10.2188/jea.JE20180249.

TEDx Talks. "Make Jokes Not War | Zev Burton | TedxGeorgetown." January 4, 2021. Video, 14:03. https://www.youtube.com/watch?v=B5ZiuyjDG84&list=ULOQn6mdZXYWw&index=517.

TEDx Talks. "The Standup Strategist: Leading with Humour | Jamie Anderson | TedxBreda." May 10, 2018. Video, 12:17. https://www.youtube.com/watch?v=RQ7W8580uHg.

CHAPTER 9: HUMOR IS HOW WE ALL SURVIVE

Miller, Michael, William F. Fry. "The Effect of Mirthful Laughter on the Human Cardiovascular System." *Medical Hypotheses* 73, no 5 (November 2009): 636-39. https://doi.org/10.1016/j.mehy.2009.02.044.

O'Neill, Tom, dir. *The History of Comedy*. Season 1, episode 1, "F***ing Funny." Aired February 9, 2017, on CNN. https://www.cnn.com/shows/history-of-comedy.

Recovery Brands LLC. "The Stigma of Mental Illness." Accessed January 30, 2021. https://www.mentalhelp.net/aware/the-stigma-of-mental-illness/.

Zenovich, Marina, dir. *Robin Williams: Come inside My Mind*. October 28, 2018, on HBO. https://www.hbo.com/documentaries/robin-williams-come-inside-my-mind.